# CONTENTS

# THE MAGICAL WORLD OF HARRY POTTER

ON THE 26TH JUNE 1997 *Harry Potter and the Philosopher's Stone* was published in the United Kingdom. In 1998, it was published as *Harry Potter and the Sorcerer's Stone* in the United States, and since then the Harry Potter books have been breaking records, selling over 450 million copies across the world, and have been translated into 80 different languages.

To celebrate twenty years of Harry Potter, explore an extraordinary collection of magical artefacts featured in the British Library's exhibition, *Harry Potter: A History of Magic*.

The exhibition is centred around the Hogwarts curriculum, uncovering the myths and folklore at the very heart of the Harry Potter series. In the pages that follow you will find carefully sourced items uncovered by a team of curators at the British Library, secured from within their own collection, as well as a handful of different institutions and private owners from around the world.

Join the curators on their journey and uncover…

✦ *Magical activities* to try at home

✦ *The tombstone of the man thought to be behind the making of the actual Philosopher's Stone*

✦ *Beautiful artwork by Jim Kay taken from the illustrated editions of Harry Potter,*
*including sketches, studies and final artwork of Hogwarts Professors, magical creatures and much more*

✦ *A very special note that helped this journey begin*

✦ *Never-before-seen material from J.K. Rowling's personal collection, including illustrations and handwritten drafts*

A MAGICAL WORLD AWAITS YOU…

# ❧ THE JOURNEY ❧

> *Harry felt a great leap of excitement. He didn't know what he was going to – but it had to be better than what he was leaving behind.*

HARRY POTTER AND THE PHILOSOPHER'S STONE

J.K. ROWLING FIRST HAD the idea for Harry Potter while delayed on a train travelling from Manchester to London in 1990. Over the next five years she planned the seven books in the award-winning series and in 1995 she finally found a home for them at Bloomsbury. Harry Potter's journey had only just begun . . .

## A CRITICAL MOMENT FOR
## THE PHILOSOPHER'S STONE

Prior to being accepted for publication by Bloomsbury, the manuscript of *Harry Potter and the Philosopher's Stone* was famously offered to some eight publishers, all of whom rejected it. The Bloomsbury editorial staff presented J.K. Rowling's manuscript to their colleagues in the form of a scroll, and filled it with Smarties, a nod to the leading children's book award at that time (the Smarties Prize). Nigel Newton, founder and Chief Executive of Bloomsbury, took the scroll home and gave it to his eight-year-old daughter, Alice.

Alice read the chapters, which went as far as Diagon Alley, and then gave her verdict, as preserved in this charming note. For long after she pestered her father to bring home the remainder of the manuscript. Alice's intervention was crucial: at the following day's acquisitions meeting, of which he was chairman, Nigel Newton approved editor Barry Cunningham's proposal that *The Philosopher's Stone* be published by Bloomsbury, leading to what is widely regarded as the most successful venture in children's publishing history.

> The excitment in this book made me Feel warm inside. I think it is possibly one of the best books an 8/9 yearold could read

*Reader's report of Alice Newton, aged eight, on Harry Potter and the Philosopher's Stone*

NIGEL NEWTON

# THE AUTHOR'S SYNOPSIS

THIS ORIGINAL SYNOPSIS of *Harry Potter and the Philosopher's Stone* was included along with the opening chapters, when it was submitted to Bloomsbury. The descriptions of the lessons at Hogwarts in this synopsis make learning magic sound incredibly exciting. The text summarises what makes Harry Potter's world so fascinating and it captured the interest of the Bloomsbury editorial team.

*Synopsis of Harry Potter and the Philosopher's Stone by J.K. Rowling (1995)*

J.K. ROWLING

---

Synopsis

Harry Potter lives with his aunt, uncle and cousin because his parents died in a car-crash - or so he has always been told. The Dursleys don't like Harry asking questions; in fact, they don't seem to like anything about him, especially the very odd things that keep happening around him (which Harry himself can't explain).

The Dursleys' greatest fear is that Harry will discover the truth about himself, so when letters start arriving for him near his eleventh birthday, he isn't allowed to read them. However, the Dursleys aren't dealing with an ordinary postman, and at midnight on Harry's birthday the gigantic Rubeus Hagrid breaks down the door to make sure Harry gets to read his post at last. Ignoring the horrified Dursleys, Hagrid informs Harry that he is a wizard, and the letter he gives Harry explains that he is expected at Hogwarts School of Witchcraft and Wizardry in a month's time.

To the Dursleys' fury, Hagrid also reveals the truth about Harry's past. Harry did not receive the scar on his forehead in a car-crash; it is really the mark of the great dark sorcerer Voldemort, who killed Harry's mother and father but mysteriously couldn't kill him, even though he was a baby at the time. Harry is famous among the witches and wizards who live in secret all over the country because Harry's miraculous survival marked Voldemort's downfall.

So Harry, who has never had friends or family worth the name, sets off for a new life in the wizarding world. He takes a trip to London with Hagrid to buy his Hogwarts equipment (robes, wand, cauldron, beginners' draft and potion kit) and shortly afterwards, sets off for Hogwarts from Kings Cross Station (platform nine and three quarters) to follow in his parents' footsteps.

Harry makes friends with Ronald Weasley (sixth in his family to go to Hogwarts and tired of having to use second-hand spellbooks) and Hermione Granger (cleverest girl in the year and the only person in the class to know all the uses of dragon's blood). Together, they have their first lessons in magic - astonomy up on the tallest tower at two in the morning, herbology out in the greenhouses where the mandrakes and wolfsbane are kept, potions down in the dungeons with the loathsome Severus Snape. Harry, Ron and Hermione discover the school's secret passageways, learn how to deal with Peeves the poltergeist and how to tackle an angry mountain troll: best of all, Harry becomes a star player at Quidditch (wizard football played on broomsticks).

What interests Harry and his friends most, though, is why the corridor on the third floor is so heavily guarded. Following up a clue dropped by Hagrid (who, when he is not delivering letters, is Hogwarts' gamekeeper), they discover that the only Philosopher's Stone in existance is being kept at Hogwarts, a stone with powers to give limitless wealth and eternal life. Harry, Ron and Hermione seem to be the only people who have realised that Snape the potions master is planning to steal the stone – and what terrible things it could do in the wrong hands. For the Philospher's Stone is all that is needed to bring Voldemort back to full strength and power... it seems Harry has come to Hogwarts to meet his parents' killer face to face – with no idea how he survived last time...

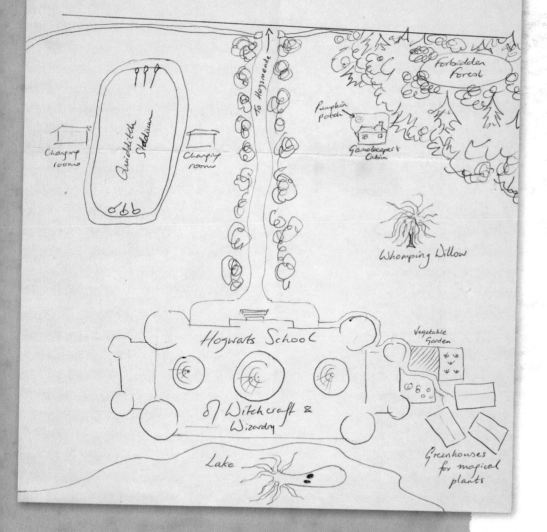

Within the sketch (handwritten annotations):

N
W — E
S

Forbidden forest is massive, stretches out o) sight.
Southern approach over lake (castle stands on high cliff above lake/loch) — station's on other side)
To reach the school by stagecoach, go right round lake to front entrance at North.
Giant squid in lake.
Seats all around Quidditch pitch — 3 long poles with hoops on at either end.
There can be other trees/bushes dotted around lawns but Whomping Willow must stand out.

Forbidden Forest

Quidditch Stadium

Changing rooms

Changing rooms

To Hogsmeade

Pumpkin patch

Gamekeeper's Cabin

Whomping Willow

Hogwarts School

of Witchcraft & Wizardry

Vegetable Garden

Greenhouses for magical plants

Lake

*Sketch of Hogwarts by J.K. Rowling*
BLOOMSBURY

# SKETCH OF HOGWARTS

THIS ANNOTATED SKETCH by J.K. Rowling shows the layout of Hogwarts School of Witchcraft and Wizardry, complete with the giant squid that lives in the lake. In an accompanying note addressed to her editor, J.K. Rowling writes, '*This is the layout as I've always imagined it*'. The positioning of various buildings and trees are all integral to the storylines of the Harry Potter books. Plot and place are tied up together throughout the series. J.K. Rowling notes that the '*Whomping Willow must stand out*', recognising its significance in *Harry Potter and the Chamber of Secrets* and *Harry Potter and the Prisoner of Azkaban*.

# HOGWARTS PROFESSORS

At the heart of Hogwarts School of Witchcraft and Wizardry are the teachers that reside there. Both Albus (which means 'white' in Latin) Percival Wulfric Brian Dumbledore and Professor Minerva McGonagall play a key role in Harry Potter's time at Hogwarts. In the following portraits by Jim Kay, Dumbledore holds a bag of what look like sherbet lemons, gazing off into the distance, while Professor McGonagall is dressed in dark green, her hair drawn back in a bun, with her glasses low on her nose.

*Portrait of Professor Albus Dumbledore by Jim Kay*
BLOOMSBURY

PROF. ALBUS DUMBLEDORE

PROF. MINERVA McGONAGALL

# HARRY POTTER AND THE DURSLEYS

*Drawing of Harry Potter and the Dursleys by J.K. Rowling (1991)*

J.K. ROWLING

> *Mr and Mrs Dursley, of number four, Privet Drive, were proud to say that they were perfectly normal, thank you very much.*

HARRY POTTER AND THE PHILOSOPHER'S STONE

OUR VERY FIRST INTRODUCTION to Harry Potter is outside his uncle's house at number four, Privet Drive, as Hagrid and Professors Dumbledore and McGonagall discuss his future. This early drawing by J.K. Rowling, made several years before *Harry Potter and the Philosopher's Stone* was published, depicts the unlikely family together.

> *'Early on I used to draw for the pleasure of seeing what I was imagining ... I had this urge to actually see these characters that I was carrying around everywhere in my mind.'*

J.K. ROWLING, 2017

Harry, despite his misery at the Dursleys', is the only one smiling. Dudley Dursley stands beside him, arms folded. Aunt Petunia and Uncle Vernon stand behind the two boys, Aunt Petunia's hand grasping Dudley's shoulder.

*Portrait of Professor McGonagall by Jim Kay*

BLOOMSBURY

# THE HOGWARTS EXPRESS

*A scarlet steam engine was waiting next to a platform packed with people. A sign overhead said Hogwarts Express, 11 o'clock.*

HARRY POTTER AND THE PHILOSOPHER'S STONE

THIS ILLUSTRATION BY JIM KAY is the artwork that features on the front cover of the illustrated *Harry Potter and the Philosopher's Stone*. Jim Kay uses a selection of different techniques to create his artwork. Images may start as a quick charcoal sketch or a detailed pencil drawing. He then works up colour in either oil or watercolour, and sometimes digitally.

This illustration shows the busy platform nine and three-quarters at King's Cross as students are boarding the iconic Hogwarts Express. Harry Potter appears, standing with his loaded trolley and Hedwig amidst the hustle and bustle.

The Hogwarts Express has a fire-breathing animal head decorating the top of its chimney and a shining bright light, while a small winged hog sits at the very front of the train.

*Platform Nine and Three-Quarters by Jim Kay*

BLOOMSBURY

# POTIONS AND ALCHEMY

*The ancient study of alchemy is concerned with making the Philosopher's Stone, a legendary substance with astonishing powers. The Stone will transform any metal into pure gold. It also produces the Elixir of Life, which will make the drinker immortal.* HARRY POTTER AND THE PHILOSOPHER'S STONE

STUDENTS OF ALCHEMY are usually interested in three things: finding the Philosopher's Stone; discovering the key to everlasting youth; and unearthing the secret behind changing the properties of metal into gold or silver. But to truly understand the science of alchemy, first you must understand the art of potions …

*Portrait of Professor Snape by Jim Kay*
BLOOMSBURY

People have been making potions for thousands upon thousands of years. The word potion is taken from the Latin word *potio*, which means 'drink'. Potions can be used for a multitude of reasons but they are often used as a medicine, poison or drug. Although not all potions are successful, this has not stopped people attempting to create them. Potions to heal a broken bone, potions to make you reveal the truth, potions to make someone fall deeply in love – people will try a magical mixture for just about everything and anything.

## PROFESSOR SEVERUS SNAPE

### PROFESSOR OF: POTIONS

(AND LATER DEFENCE AGAINST THE DARK ARTS)

APPEARANCE: Professor Snape is described as having greasy black hair, a hooked nose and sallow skin. His eyes are said to be black, cold and empty.

DID YOU KNOW: Marauders Moony, Wormtail, Padfoot and Prongs had a nickname for Professor Snape when they were students together at Hogwarts – Snivellus.

### A PUZZLING PROFESSOR

*Although Professor Snape is described as being 'disliked by everybody' in the early stages of Harry's time at Hogwarts, we later discover that appearances can often be deceptive. As Snape's own personal story unravels he is cast in a different light, which allows us to re-examine his previous actions and perhaps perceive them in a different way.*

*Cruel, sarcastic and disliked by everybody except the students from his own house (Slytherin), Snape taught Potions.*

HARRY POTTER AND THE CHAMBER OF SECRETS

PROF.
SEVERUS                                    SNAPE

# POTIONS CLASS

POTIONS IS ONE OF SEVERAL subjects compulsory for all Hogwarts students.

---

*'Double Potions with the Slytherins,' said Ron. 'Snape's Head of Slytherin house. They say he always favours them – we'll be able to see if it's true.'*

HARRY POTTER AND THE PHILOSOPHER'S STONE

---

This book shows the image of a Potions master and his students. *Ortus Sanitatis* (Latin for 'The Garden of Health') is the first printed encyclopedia of natural history, featuring plants, animals, birds, fish and stones. In this image the Potions master is clutching a stick in his left hand, while his assistant is holding open a book of recipes. It's questionable how much attention some of the pupils are paying to their teacher!

### DID YOU KNOW?

*This woodcut engraving was coloured by hand. Woodcut is a form of printing where the artist carves an image into the surface of a block of wood and then covers it in ink. The block is then pressed on to a piece of paper to reveal the image.*

*Jacob Meydenbach, Ortus Sanitatis (Strasbourg, 1491)*

BRITISH LIBRARY

## ACTIVITY

### POTION MAKING

The art of potion making can take several years to perfect. However, you can have a go at concocting some potions without attending a single Potions class.

TO MAKE A SWIRLING, IRIDESCENT POTION that you can drink, add a few drops of food colouring (any colour you like) to a glass of lemon-lime soda, add a little edible gold sparkle powder (for decorating cakes) and stir well. Let it settle and it will be a clear, coloured potion. But when you stir it, the gold will swirl around, making it look as though the potion is magical.

TO MAKE A COLOUR-CHANGING POTION, chop up some red cabbage and put it in a bowl. Next ask an adult to help you cover it with hot water and leave for 15 minutes. Then pour the mixture through a sieve and keep the liquid. You will be left with a purple potion. To change the colour, add lemon juice or vinegar to turn it red, or bicarbonate of soda to turn it green or blue. Put a spoonful of the original potion in a glass and watch it turn red as you top it up with lemon-lime soda. You can drink this – and it won't even taste of cabbage!

'...I can teach you how to bottle fame, brew glory, even stopper death – if you aren't as big a bunch of dunderheads as I usually have to teach.' PROFESSOR SNAPE – HARRY POTTER AND THE PHILOSOPHER'S STONE

# BEZOAR STONES

'A bezoar is a stone taken from the stomach of a goat and it will save you from most poisons.'

PROFESSOR SNAPE – HARRY POTTER AND THE PHILOSOPHER'S STONE

BEZOAR STONES really do exist. The stones are found in the stomach of certain animals and are made up of a collection of undigested fibre. They vary in size but are usually roughly the size of a hen's egg. Taken from the Persian word for antidote, bezoars were first introduced into medieval Europe by Arabic physicians. They have been found in the guts of cows and even elephants, but mostly they come from the 'bezoar goat'.

*A bezoar stone in a gold filigree case*
SCIENCE MUSEUM

It was thought that the stones would cure you from almost any poison and even though not everyone believed in their magical properties, bezoar stones remained popular well into the 18th century. Wealthy collectors such as popes, kings and noblemen spent huge amounts of money so that they could have the best stones. According to *A Compleat History of Druggs*, the strength of the bezoar stone depends on the animal that produces it.

In *The Half-Blood Prince*, Harry notices an instruction in his copy of *Advanced Potion-Making* while in Professor Slughorn's Potions class:

## Just shove a bezoar down their throats

HARRY POTTER AND THE HALF-BLOOD PRINCE

He does exactly that when Ron drinks some poisoned mead, and saves his friend's life. However, although this worked for Harry and Ron you should *never* try this at home!

## FACT

### ANIMALS

In the past, different parts of animals were used in potions. People thought that you would gain characteristics of the animal by doing this. One such invisibility potion involved adding a black cat to your recipe. Black cats are almost impossible to see at night and so it was believed that the drinker would become hard to see.

*Pierre Pomet, A Compleat History of Druggs, 2nd edn (London, 1725)*

BRITISH LIBRARY

# An Apothecary's Sign

'*...it is a monstrous thing, to slay a unicorn,' said Firenze. 'Only one who has nothing to lose, and everything to gain, would commit such a crime. The blood of a unicorn will keep you alive, even if you are an inch from death, but at a terrible price.*'

Firenze – Harry Potter and the Philosopher's Stone

Throughout history, the blood, hair and horns of unicorns were thought to possess powerful medicinal properties. People would pay huge sums of money for these rare and precious artefacts. This 18th-century sign from an apothecary's shop uses the prized image of a unicorn. Images and pictures were frequently used to identify shops, as a large portion of the population would have been illiterate at the time.

Carved in oak with a real ivory horn, the sign symbolised to customers that this apothecary was able to provide rare and exotic cures. Of course, it wasn't actually a real unicorn horn at all (that would be impossible!), but was in fact made from the tusk of a narwhal. Known as the 'unicorns of the sea', narwhals were hunted for their valuable tusks which were frequently sold as unicorn horns because of their similarity in look and texture.

## FACT

### WHAT IS AN APOTHECARY?

An apothecary is a term used throughout history to describe someone who prepared and sold medicine. The study of herbal and chemical ingredients led the way to modern sciences, and today we refer to people in this line of work as pharmacists or chemists.

### DID YOU KNOW?

*Up until recently scientists weren't sure why narwhals have these tusks. However, new research suggests that the tusks are sensory organs, which pick up changes in the whale's environment, alerting them to food and other whales.*

*A pharmacy sign in the shape of a unicorn's head (18th century)*
SCIENCE MUSEUM

# POTION BOTTLES

This image by Jim Kay, for the illustrated edition of *Harry Potter and the Philosopher's Stone*, shows the beautiful detail of a selection of potion bottles. Each bottle seems to be full of life. What might these enchanting potion bottles hold? Skele-Gro to help re-grow bones? Felix Felicis to bring good luck to the potion maker? Or perhaps some Polyjuice Potion which allows the drinker to take on the appearance of someone else …

*Potion bottles by Jim Kay*

BLOOMSBURY

*The shadowy walls were lined with shelves of large glass jars, in which floated all manner of revolting things Harry didn't really want to know the name of at the moment.*

HARRY POTTER AND THE CHAMBER OF SECRETS

'*You are here to learn the subtle science and exact art of* **potion-making** …'
HARRY POTTER AND THE PHILOSOPHER'S STONE

# THE BATTERSEA CAULDRON

---

*The sun shone brightly on a stack of cauldrons outside the nearest shop.* Cauldrons – All Sizes – Copper, Brass, Pewter, Silver – Self-Stirring – Collapsible *said a sign hanging over them.*

HARRY POTTER AND THE PHILOSOPHER'S STONE

---

*Neville had somehow managed to melt Seamus's cauldron into a twisted blob and their potion was seeping across the stone floor, burning holes in people's shoes.*

HARRY POTTER AND THE PHILOSOPHER'S STONE

CAULDRONS ARE one of the best-known objects associated with witchcraft. They probably came in all shapes and sizes and were used for lots of different purposes, including creating potions.

This cauldron is almost three thousand years old, and was created by melding together seven plates of sheet bronze with two handles fastened to its rim. It was found in the River Thames more than two millennia after it had been made.

We can't know for certain if witches used this cauldron but, as it is so beautifully and carefully made, it probably belonged to a very wealthy owner.

*The Battersea cauldron (c. 800–600 BC)*
BRITISH MUSEUM

# WITCHES WITH A CAULDRON

The idea of witches surrounding a smoking cauldron has been around for centuries. However, their association with cauldrons did not actually appear in print until 1489. *On Witches and Female Fortune Tellers*, written by Ulrich Molitor, contains the earliest printed image of witches with a cauldron. Two elderly women can be seen placing a snake and a cockerel into a large flaming pot, in order to create a hailstorm. *On Witches* was so widely reproduced that it helped to shape people's ideas about how witches were supposed to behave.

In some tales cauldrons don't just hold magic potions; they can themselves be magical!

In J.K. Rowling's *The Tales of Beedle the Bard*, 'The Wizard and the Hopping Pot' tells the tale of a selfish wizard who refuses to use his magic to help Muggles with their ailments. But his cauldron is magic – it grows a foot and hops about by the wizard's side, clanking and banging and knocking around. Eventually the wizard has had enough, and as soon as he agrees to help the Muggles the cauldron quietly settles back down.

*At every house of sickness and sorrow, the wizard did his best, and gradually the cooking pot beside him stopped groaning and retching, and became quiet, shiny and clean.*

THE TALES OF BEEDLE THE BARD

*Ulrich Molitor, De laniis et phitonicis mulieribus... tractatus pulcherrimus (Cologne, 1489)*
BRITISH LIBRARY

# EDITED DRAFTS of HARRY POTTER AND THE HALF-BLOOD PRINCE

PROFESSOR SLUGHORN arrives at Hogwarts during Harry's sixth year and takes over the role of Potions Master. These two pages show annotations by J.K. Rowling and her editor on a draft of *Harry Potter and the Half-Blood Prince*.

The first page is a draft of Professor Slughorn's first Potions class, where he presents several potions to his students that Hermione, naturally, is able to identify. The asterisks indicate that the handwritten text at the bottom of the page, where Hermione talks about her favourite smells, needs to be inserted.

---

*Hermione's well-practised hand hit the air before anybody else's; Slughorn pointed at her. 'It's Veritaserum, a colourless potion that forces the drinker to tell the truth,' said Hermione.*

HARRY POTTER AND THE HALF-BLOOD PRINCE

---

'It's Veritaserum, a colourless, odourless potion that forces the drinker to tell the truth,' said Hermione.

'Very good, very good!' said Slughorn, beaming at her. 'Now, this one here is pretty well-known... featured in a few Ministry leaflets lately, too... who can -?'

Hermione's hand was fastest once more.

'It's Polyjuice Potion, sir,' she said.

Harry, too, had recognised the slow-bubbling, mud-like substance in the second cauldron, but did not resent Hermione getting the credit for answering the question; she, after all, was the one who had succeeded in making it, back in their second year.

'Excellent, excellent! Now, this one here... yes, my dear?' said Slughorn, now looking slightly bemused, as Hermione's hand punched the air again.

'It's Amortentia!'

'It is indeed. It seems almost foolish to ask,' said Slughorn, who was looking mightily impressed, 'but I assume you know what it does?'

'It's the most powerful love potion in the world!' said Hermione.

'Quite right! You recognised it, I suppose, by its distinctive mother-of-pearl sheen?'

'And the steam rising in characteristic spirals,' said Hermione. ✳

'May I ask your name, my dear?' *said Slughorn, ~~at the pause~~ ignoring these signs of embarrassment.*

'Hermione Granger, sir.'

'Granger? Granger? Can you possibly be related to Hector Dagworth-Granger, who founded the Most Extraordinary Society of Potioneers?'

'No, I don't think so, sir. I'm Muggle-born, you see.'

*he continued pointing at the [cauldron] of [...] cauldron nearest the Ravenclaw table*

*✳ 'and it's supposed to smell differently to each of us, according to what attracts us, and I can smell freshly-mown grass and new parchment and —' But she turned slightly pink and did not complete the sentence ~~they took~~*

175

'How many times have we been through this?' she said wearily. 'There's a big difference between needing to use the room and wanting to see what Malfoy needs it for –'

'Harry might need the same thing as Malfoy and not know he needs it!' said Ron. 'Harry, if you took a bit of Felix, you might suddenly feel the same need as Malfoy –'

'Harry, don't go wasting the rest of that Potion! You'll need all the luck you can get if Dumbledore takes you along with him to destroy a,' she dropped her voice to a whisper, 'horcrux, so you just stop encouraging him to take a slug of Felix every time he wants something!' she added sternly to Ron.

'Couldn't we make some more?' Ron asked Harry, ignoring Hermione. 'It'd be great to have a stock of it... have a look in the book...'

Harry pulled his copy of *Advanced Potion-Making* out of his bag and looked up *Felix Felicis*.

'Blimey, it's seriously complicated,' he said, running an eye down the list of ingredients. 'And it takes six months... you've got to let it stew...'

'Dammit,' said Ron.

Harry was about to put his book away again when he noticed that the corner of a page turned down; turning to it, he saw the 'Sectumsempra' spell, captioned 'for Enemies,' that he had marked a few weeks previously. He had still not found out what it did, mainly because he did not want to test it around Hermione, but he was considering trying it out on McLaggen next time he came up behind him unawares.

The only person who was not particularly pleased to see Katie Bell back at school was Dean Thomas, because he would no longer be required to fill her place as Chaser. He took the blow stoically enough when Harry told him, merely grunting and

495

In this draft Harry consults his copy of *Advanced Potion-Making*. He notices one of the Half-Blood Prince's spells, '*Sectumsempra*', only later on realising the danger of using an unknown spell.

*Harry was about to put his book away again when he noticed the corner of the page folded down; turning to it, he saw the* Sectumsempra *spell, captioned 'For Enemies', that he had marked a few weeks previously.*

HARRY POTTER AND THE HALF-BLOOD PRINCE

*Draft of Harry Potter and the Half-Blood Prince, annotated by J.K. Rowling and her editor (c. 2004–2005)*

BLOOMSBURY

# NICOLAS FLAMEL, ALCHEMIST

IN THEIR FIRST YEAR at Hogwarts, Harry, Hermione and Ron spend a huge amount of time trying to find out anything they can about Nicolas Flamel. Their efforts pay off when they eventually discover that he is the only known maker of the Philosopher's Stone.

*There have been many reports of the Philosopher's Stone over the centuries, but the only Stone currently in existence belongs to Mr Nicolas Flamel, the noted alchemist and opera-lover. Mr Flamel, who celebrated his six hundred and sixty-fifth birthday last year, enjoys a quiet life in Devon with his wife, Perenelle (six hundred and fifty-eight).*

HARRY POTTER AND THE PHILOSOPHER'S STONE

Nicolas Flamel was a real person, and though once thought to have been an alchemist, he didn't actually create a Philosopher's Stone. He was in fact a landlord and some sources describe him as a bookseller. Flamel spent his life in Paris and died in 1418. This illustration shows a memorial to the Holy Innocents commissioned by Nicolas and his wife Perenelle, with the Flamels praying at the top beside the saints.

*Watercolour illustrations to a memoir of Nicolas Flamel and his wife (France, 18th century)*

BRITISH LIBRARY

COMMENT LES INNO-
=CENS FVRENT OCCIS
PAR LE COMMANDEMĒT
DV ROY HERODES

# Burial

The real Nicolas Flamel was buried in the church of Saint-Jacques-de-la-Boucherie in Paris; his grave was marked by this medieval tombstone, which is 58 cm high and inscribed in French. The top of the tombstone shows Christ with Saints Peter and Paul, along with the sun and moon; the deceased Flamel is shown underneath the inscription.

*Tombstone of Nicolas Flamel
(Paris, 15th century)*
MUSÉE NATIONAL DU MOYEN-ÂGE

'... it really is like going to bed after a very, very long day. After all, to the well-organised mind, death is but the next great adventure.'

PROFESSOR DUMBLEDORE – HARRY POTTER AND THE PHILOSOPHER'S STONE

# QUIRRELL AND THE PHILOSOPHER'S STONE

THIS EARLY DRAFT of Chapter 17 of *Harry Potter and the Philosopher's Stone* was handwritten by J.K. Rowling. Most of the dialogue that appears here remains the same as the published text, but in this draft Harry is given this defiant line:

---

*'You haven't got the stone yet ... Dumbledore will be here soon. He'll stop you.'*

---

The confrontation between Harry and Quirrell was re-organised during the editorial process and as a result the line was cut.

Chapter Seventeen
The Man with Two Faces.

It was Quirrell.

"*You*!" said Harry.

Quirrell smiled, and his face wasn't twitching at all.

"Me," he said calmly.

"But I thought — Snape —"

"Severus?" Quirrell laughed and it wasn't his usual quivering treble either, but cold and sharp. "Yes, Severus does seem the type, doesn't he? So useful to have him swooping around like an overgrown bat. Next to him, who would suspect me? P — p — poor st — st — stuttering P — P — Professor Quirrell."

"But he tried to kill me —"

"No, no, no," said Quirrell. "*I* was trying to kill you. Your friend Miss Granger accidentally knocked me over as she rushed to set fire to Snape. It broke my eye contact with you. Another few seconds and I'd have got you off that broom. I'd have managed it before then if Snape hadn't been muttering a counter-curse, trying to save you."

"He was trying to save me?"

"Of course," said Quirrell coolly. "Why do you think he wanted to referee your next match? He was trying to make sure I didn't do it again. Funny, really ... he needn't have bothered. I couldn't do anything with Dumbledore watching. All the other teachers thought Snape was trying to stop Gryffindor winning, he did make a fool of himself ... and he needn't have bothered and what a waste of time, when after all that I'm going to kill you tonight."

Quirrell snapped his fingers. Ropes sprang out of thin air and wrapped themselves tightly around Harry.

"Now, you wait there, Potter, while I examine this interesting mirror —"

It was only then that Harry realised what was standing behind Quirrell. It was the Mirror of Erised.

"You haven't got the stone yet —" said Harry desperately. "Dumbledore will be here soon. He'll stop you —"

"For someone who's about to die, you're very talkative, Potter," said Quirrell, feeling his way around the Mirror's frame. "This mirror is the key to finding the stone, it won't take me long — and Dumbledore's in London, I'll be far away by the time he gets here —"

All Harry could think of was to keep Quirrell talking.

"That troll at Hallowe'en —"

"Yes, I let it in. I was hoping some foolhardy student would get themselves killed by it, to give me time to get the stone. Unfortunately, Snape found out. I think see what was guarding that ghost with ~~his head hanging off~~ the loose head tipped him off. Snape came straight to the third floor corridor to head me off ... and you didn't get killed by the troll! That was why I tried to finish you at the Quidditch match — but blow me if I didn't fail again."

Quirrell rapped the Mirror of Erised impatiently.

"Dratted thing ... trust Dumbledore to come up with something like this ..." He stared hungrily into the mirror. "I see me stone," he said. "I'm presenting it to my Master ... but where is it?"

He went back to feeling his way around the mirror.

B

~~A sudden thought struck~~ Harry's ~~B~~ mind was racing. at this moment,"

"What I want more than anything else in the world," he thought, "is to find the stone before Quirrell does. So if I look in the mirror, I should see myself finding it — which means I'll see where it's hidden. But how can I look without him realising what I'm up to? ~~&~~ I've got to play for time ..."

"I saw you and Snape in the forest," he blurted out.

"Yes," said Quirrell idly, walking around the mirror to look at the back. "He was onto me. Trying to find out how far I'd got. He suspected me all along. Tried to frighten me — as though he could scare me, ~~with~~ ~~me~~ ~~I had~~ Lord Voldemort ~~behind me~~ on my side."

"But Snape always seemed to hate me so much —"

"Oh, he does," Quirrell said casually. "Heavens, yes. He was at ~~school~~ Hogwarts with your father, didn't you know? They loathed each other. But he ~~never~~ didn't want you dead."

"And that warning burned into my bed —"

"Yes, that was me," said Quirrell, now ~~&~~ feeling the Mirror's clawed feet. "I heard you and Weasley in my class, talking about Philosopher's Stones. I ~~thought you~~ thought you might try and interfere. ~~So~~ Pity you didn't heed my warning, isn't it? Curiosity has led you to your doom, Potter."

"But I heard you a few days ago, ~~I thought~~ sobbing — I thought Snape was threatening you —"

For the first time, a spasm of fear flitted across Quirrell's face.

"Sometimes —" he said, "I find it hard to follow my Master's instructions — he is a great man and I am weak —"

"You mean he was there in the classroom with you?" Harry gasped.

"He is with me wherever I go," said Quirrell softly. "I met ~~him~~ with him when I ~~travelled~~ round the world, a ~~&~~ foolish young man, full of ~~ridiculous~~ ridiculous ideas about good and evil. Lord Voldemort showed me how wrong I was. There is no good and evil. There is only power, and those too weak to seek it ... Since then, I have served him faithfully, though I have let him down many times. He has ~~had to be~~ very hard on me." Quirrell shuddered suddenly. "He does not forgive mistakes easily. When I failed to steal the stone from

*A draft of Harry Potter and the Philosopher's Stone, Chapter 17, handwritten by J.K. Rowling*

J.K. ROWLING

# SEEING FLUFFY

THIS ORIGINAL HAND-DRAWN illustration by J.K. Rowling shows Neville, Ron, Harry, Hermione and Gary (later renamed Dean, who was actually cut from this scene) coming face-to-face with a huge three-headed dog which is guarding the Philosopher's Stone.

J.K. Rowling has included details in the illustration to highlight each student's character: Neville's bunny pyjamas, Ron's freckles and Hermione's large front teeth. This drawing provides an exciting insight into how J.K. Rowling initially imagined her characters to look.

*They were looking straight into the eyes of a monstrous dog, a dog which filled the whole space between ceiling and floor. It had three heads. Three pairs of rolling, mad eyes; three noses, twitching and quivering in their direction; three drooling mouths, saliva hanging in slippery ropes from yellowish fangs.*

HARRY POTTER AND THE PHILOSOPHER'S STONE

L–R : Neville, Ron, Harry, Hermione, Gary

Chap 7. Draco Duel

### DID YOU KNOW?

*This scene was originally intended to be part of Chapter Seven, 'Draco's Duel'. However, during the editorial process the scene became Chapter Nine and was renamed 'The Midnight Duel'.*

*Pen-and-ink drawing of Harry and his friends by J.K. Rowling (1991)*

J.K. ROWLING

# CERBERUS

Cerberus features in many ancient legends. In Greek mythology, Cerberus was the monstrous, three-headed dog that guarded the gates to the Underworld.

This wood engraving by Edward Burne-Jones (1833–1898) was designed to illustrate William Morris's *The Earthly Paradise*. In this story a character named Psyche is sent on a quest to the Underworld. She has to use cakes made of honey to distract the dreaded Cerberus.

*Edward Burne-Jones and William Morris,* Psyche *throwing the honey cakes to Cerberus (c. 1880)*
BIRMINGHAM MUSEUM AND ART GALLERY

*Fluffy by Jim Kay*
BLOOMSBURY

# The Ripley Scroll

The INCREDIBLE Ripley Scroll is a mystical alchemical manuscript. It is covered in enchanting illustrations along with text called 'Verses upon the Elixer'. These verses are a recipe for creating the Philosopher's Stone.

It takes its name from George Ripley (died c. 1490) who reportedly studied alchemy, and wrote a book on how to make a Philosopher's Stone, known as *The Compound of Alchymy*. The scroll features dragons, toads and a winged bird captioned, '*The Bird of Hermes is my name / Eating my Wings to make me lame*'.

### Did you know?

*This manuscript is roughly six metres long. That's as tall as a giraffe! Because of its extraordinary length, the scroll had rarely been unrolled in living memory before the Harry Potter: A History of Magic exhibition in 2017. This is because the curators didn't have a table long enough to unroll it on!*

'You know, the Stone was really not such a wonderful thing. As much money and life as you could want! The two things most human beings would choose above all — the trouble is, humans do have a knack of choosing precisely those things which are worst for them.'

PROFESSOR DUMBLEDORE – HARRY POTTER AND THE PHILOSOPHER'S STONE

*The Ripley Scroll (England, 16th century)*
BRITISH LIBRARY

*Sections of the Ripley Scroll*

# HERBOLOGY

*Three times a week they went out to the greenhouses behind the castle to study Herbology, with a dumpy little witch called Professor Sprout, where they learnt how to take care of all the strange plants and fungi and found out what they were used for.* Harry Potter and the Philosopher's Stone

The fascinating and important study of herbology has helped us to use plants to treat illnesses for thousands of years. People carry out this practice to promote health and to uncover the medicinal properties held by plants.

Herbology is a core subject for all Hogwarts students. During these lessons, students learn how to care for plants and explore their magical properties and what they can be used for. Countless plants in the wizarding world are packed full of magical uses and can provide ingredients for potions. Mandrakes, Bubotubers and Gillyweed are among the many plants that form an essential part of any young witch or wizard's education.

## PROFESSOR POMONA SPROUT
### PROFESSOR OF: HERBOLOGY

Appearance: Professor Sprout is described as a squat little witch with grey, flyaway hair whose clothes are usually covered in earth.

Did you know: Professor Sprout was tasked with fixing up the Whomping Willow after Harry and Ron flew Mr Weasley's old Ford Anglia into it in their second year at Hogwarts.

## FACT

### MEDICINAL PLANTS

Many modern medicines are based on plants. Digoxin, used to treat heart conditions, was originally obtained from foxgloves. The painkillers morphine and codeine both come from the opium poppy. Quinine is still used to treat malaria. Aspirin is based on the chemical salicin, which is found in the bark of willow trees.

### Did you know?

*Rubbing a dock leaf on a nettle sting will soothe it. People used to think this was because a chemical in the dock leaf reacted with the stinging chemical in the nettle. However, it's just the cool sap from the dock making the sting feel better.*

*Portrait of Professor Pomona Sprout by Jim Kay*

BLOOMSBURY

# PROFESSOR SPROUT

*'– and be careful of the Venomous Tentacula, it's teething.' She gave a sharp slap to a spiky, dark red plant as she spoke, making it draw in the long feelers that had been inching sneakily over her shoulder.*

PROFESSOR SPROUT – HARRY POTTER AND THE CHAMBER OF SECRETS

*Pen-and-ink drawing of
Professor Pomona Sprout by J.K. Rowling
(30 December 1990)*

J.K. ROWLING

THIS HAND-DRAWN ILLUSTRATION by J.K. Rowling, made seven years before the publication of *Harry Potter and the Philosopher's Stone*, shows Professor Sprout surrounded by plants studied in her Herbology class. Sprout is shown in her witch's hat, with a spider hanging from its tip.

Look carefully at the plants drawn here and you'll see that a few have some unusual characteristics. Could the tendrils spilling out of the pot be the sneaky Venomous Tentacula, looking for something to grab?

## FACT

### *PLANTS THAT MOVE*

Plants do move, but most of them do it so slowly that we don't notice. However, there are a few speedy plants around. The Venus flytrap catches insects between a pair of special leaves that snap shut like a book. The sensitive plant quickly closes its delicate leaves and lets them droop down if you touch it or blow on it.

# MANDRAKE ROOTS

A real mandrake root
(England, 16th or 17th century)
SCIENCE MUSEUM

*'The Mandrake forms an essential part of most antidotes. It is also, however, dangerous. Who can tell me why?' Hermione's hand narrowly missed Harry's glasses as it shot up again. 'The cry of the Mandrake is fatal to anyone who hears it,' she said promptly.*

PROFESSOR SPROUT AND HERMIONE – HARRY POTTER AND THE CHAMBER OF SECRETS

Giovanni Cadamosto's illustrated herbal
(Italy or Germany, 15th century)
BRITISH LIBRARY

Mandrakes really do exist and their roots do resemble the human form, which has influenced many cultures to attribute special powers to the plant. According to medieval herbals, mandrakes (*Mandragora*) had great medical potential. People believed they would cure headaches, earaches, and insanity, among other ailments.

However, it was said that the roots shrieked when dug up and anyone who heard that noise went mad. People believed that the best way to harvest the plant safely was to unearth its roots with an ivory stake, attach one end of a cord to the plant and the other to a dog. The dog was then encouraged to move forward by sounding a horn (which would drown out the shrieking) or by enticing it with meat. Once the dog moved it would drag the mandrake with it.

In reality, mandrakes don't actually cry. But they are still dangerous: their leaves are poisonous and can cause hallucinations.

## FACT

### PLANTS AND NOISE

There aren't any plants that can actually make noise, but some of them seem to be able to hear! A recent study showed that if you play a recording of the noise of chomping caterpillars to various types of plant, they produce chemicals that caterpillars find unpleasant to eat, and this protects them from the grazing insects!

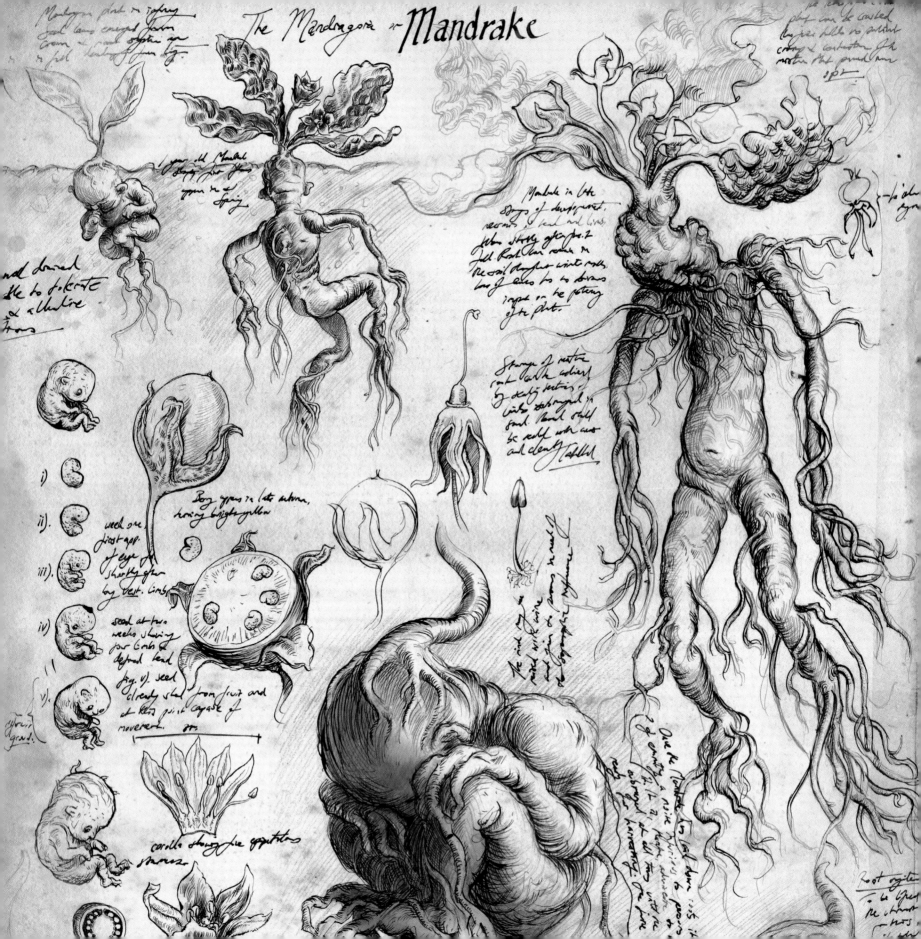

# The Mandragora or Mandrake

# A STUDY OF MANDRAKES

*Instead of roots, a small, muddy and extremely ugly baby popped out of the earth. The leaves were growing right out of his head. He had pale green, mottled skin, and was clearly bawling at the top of his lungs.*

HARRY POTTER AND THE CHAMBER OF SECRETS

THIS DRAWING by Jim Kay shows a baby mandrake alongside a fully grown adult. The roots of the plant seamlessly form the adult mandrake's body, with leaves growing from its head. The mature mandrake also has berries sprouting among the leaves, alluding to the plant's reproductive maturity. This illustration appears to be drawn from life – Jim Kay was previously a curator at the Royal Botanic Gardens, Kew – and it references the natural studies of plants that are typically found in any botanical library.

*Study of mandrakes by Jim Kay*
BLOOMSBURY

## ACTIVITY

### COLOUR-CHANGING FLOWERS

Bring some magic to your flowers with this colour-changing trick! You will need white flowers (carnations work well) and some food colouring – any colour that you like.

Half fill a glass with water and add enough food colouring to make a deep colour. Next ask an adult to help you cut a few centimetres off the bottom of the flower stems. Stand the trimmed flowers in the coloured water. Keep an eye on your flowers and watch as they begin to change over time. The longer you leave them, the deeper the new colour of the petals will become.

To make a two-coloured flower, ask an adult to split the stem of a white flower all along its length. Make sure to keep the flower at the top intact! Stand each half of the stem in a separate glass with different food colourings and watch as your two-coloured flower comes to life!

### 'MANDRAKE' AND 'WOMANDRAKE'

*Pedanius Dioscorides (died c. AD 90) was a Greek botanist and pharmacologist. Dioscorides was one of the first authors to distinguish between the male and female mandrake. In fact, this identification is based on there being more than one species of mandrake native to the Mediterranean.*

# A HERBAL

MANY PLANTS WERE researched the world over for magical healing properties. A herbal is a book of plants, which describes their appearance, properties and how they can be used to prepare ointments and medicines. Many of the wonderful herbs and potions names used in the Harry Potter books suggest links to the research done by those who dedicated their time to exploring the countless varieties of plants that fill our world.

# CULPEPER'S HERBAL

Popularly known as 'Culpeper's Herbal', this book by Nicholas Culpeper (1616–1654) was first published in 1652 as *The English Physician*. Since then it has appeared in over 100 editions, and it was the first medical book to be published in North America.

Culpeper wanted the text to be accessible to everyone, so he wrote it in English rather than the traditional Latin. His herbal provided a detailed list of native medicinal herbs, matched with specific illnesses, and prescribed the most effective forms of treatment and when to take them.

J.K. Rowling consulted Culpeper when researching the Harry Potter series.

*'I've got two copies of Culpeper, one a cheap edition I bought second-hand years ago and one beautiful version I was given by Bloomsbury.'*

J.K. ROWLING, 2017

*Culpeper's The English Physician; and Complete Herbal (London, 1789)*

BRITISH LIBRARY

DID YOU KNOW?

*Culpeper was an unlicensed apothecary, and was disliked by the medical profession, who believed that they should be the only ones to practise medicine in London. He came into conflict with the College of Physicians, and in 1642 he was apparently tried (but acquitted) for practising witchcraft.*

# ELIZABETH BLACKWELL'S CURIOUS HERBAL

*A Curious Herbal* is a book with an incredible history. This work was illustrated, engraved and hand-coloured by Elizabeth Blackwell (1707–1758), in order to raise funds to have her husband, Alexander, released from a debtors' prison (a prison for people who are unable to pay back money they owe).

The book was released in weekly parts between 1737 and 1739 and contained 500 images. Elizabeth drew the images at Chelsea Physic Garden in London, and took them to Alexander in prison, to identify each of the plants.

Through the sales of her book, Elizabeth raised enough money to release her husband. However, Alexander eventually left for Sweden, where he was executed for treason, having become involved in a political conspiracy. Elizabeth died alone in England in 1758.

## FACT

### HERBALS

Civilisations all over the world have been producing herbals for thousands of years. They were very important books, because for many centuries they contained the only medical advice available. As well as describing medicinal uses of plants, herbals often contained 'magical' information. People believed that problems with a particular body part could be treated by using a plant with a similar shape to that part. So lung problems could be treated with the plant lungwort, which has spotty leaves the same shape as lungs.

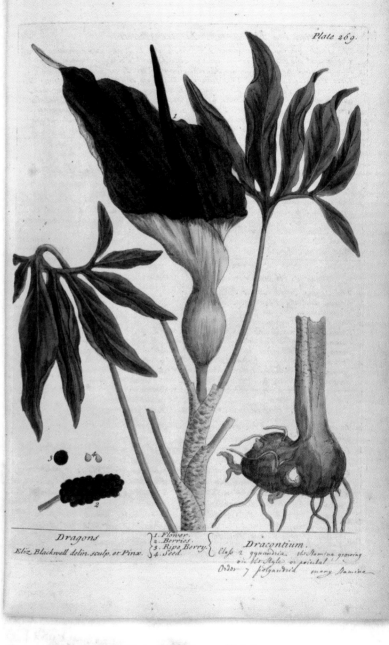

*Dracontium, in Elizabeth Blackwell, A Curious Herbal, containing five hundred cuts of the most useful plants which are now used in the practice of Physic, 2 vols (London, 1737–39)*

BRITISH LIBRARY

# SNAKEROOT

DURING THE MIDDLE AGES, students of herbology often kept detailed notes for their own use, recording and illustrating the properties of different plants.

This magnificently decorated herbal was made in Lombardy (northern Italy) around 1440, most probably for a wealthy owner. It contains life-like drawings of various plants, each with a short note explaining their names. There are images of snakeroot, along with some of its Latin names including, *'dragontea'*, *'serpentaria'* and *'viperina'*. It was claimed that this plant could cure a snake bite.

A hissing green snake curls round its root while to the left sits a snarling dragon, with a forked tongue and an elaborately knotted tail, called in Latin *'Draco magnus'*.

### DID YOU KNOW?

The term 'snakeroot' is used today to refer to various plants with medicinal qualities, such as plantain, which is widely believed to speed up the healing process when applied to a wound.

*Snakeroot in a herbal (Italy, 15th century)*
BRITISH LIBRARY

# A Remedy for Snake Bite

There was a time when people believed that one of the most effective remedies for snake bite was the flowering plant, centaury. According to this 12th-century manuscript, the two plants known as *Centauria major* and *Centauria minor* (greater and lesser centaury) were named after the centaur, Chiron. In Greek mythology, Chiron was the greatest of all centaurs, renowned as a physician, astrologer and oracle. Among his pupils was Asclepius, the god of medicine and healing, who had been rescued as a baby and was taken to Chiron to be raised.

In this pen-and-ink drawing, Chiron is shown handing over the two plants in question to the toga-wearing Asclepius. A snake is seen slithering away from under their feet.

*Centaury in a herbal (England, 12th century)*
BRITISH LIBRARY

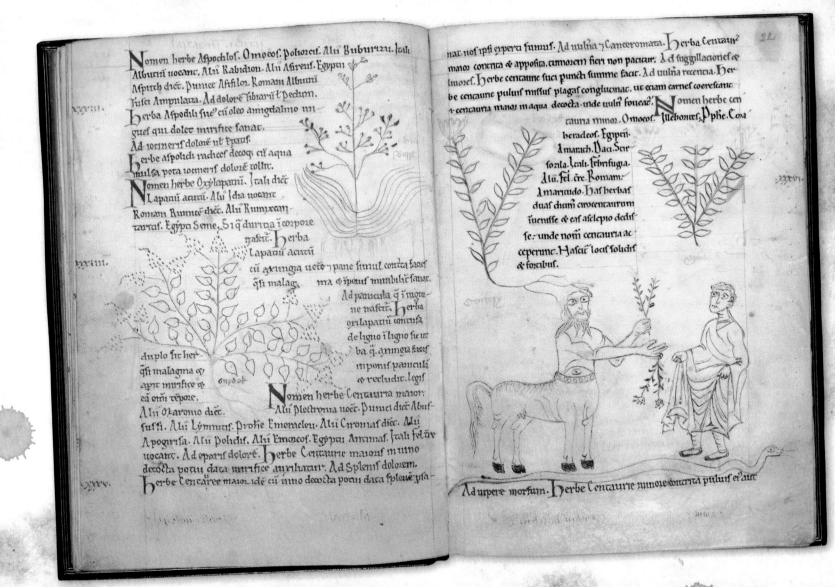

# A STUDY OF GNOMES

*It was small and leathery-looking, with a large, knobbly, bald head exactly like a potato. Ron held it at arm's length as it kicked out at him with its horny little feet ...*

HARRY POTTER AND THE CHAMBER OF SECRETS

HAVE YOU EVER SEEN A GNOME? Jolly-faced, big-bellied and usually with bright, rosy cheeks, they sit in people's gardens as a decoration. However, in the magical world, they are somewhat different. Gnomes, or *Gernumbli gardensi* to give them their scientific name, grow to be roughly one foot tall. They burrow gnome holes in gardens, dig up roots and create unsightly mounds of earth.

These detailed drawings by Jim Kay clearly show the knobbliness of the creature's head and its horned feet. The ugliness of these creatures, with their potato-like heads and dim expressions of confusion, is well captured in Kay's studies.

### DID YOU KNOW?

*Gnomes were once believed to represent earth, one of the four elements thought to be the forces of nature at that time (the others were fire, air and water). They avoided contact with humans and were often the guardians of treasure under the earth.*

# MAGICAL GARDENING IMPLEMENTS

No magical garden is complete without the right tools with which to take care of it. These gardening implements, made from bone and antler, were used specifically for sowing and harvesting plants and would have been used for thousands of years.

Many plants are harvested not only for their medicinal qualities but for their alleged supernatural powers. Some people believe that the rituals involved in gathering them are extremely important. For the users of these implements, it was essential that they were formed entirely from natural resources so that they did not corrupt the plants being harvested.

*Preparatory and final artwork of gnomes by Jim Kay*
BLOOMSBURY

*Gardening implements made from antler and bone*
THE MUSEUM OF WITCHCRAFT AND MAGIC

The materials used to make them also had symbolic importance. Tools shaped from antlers, grown above the head, were thought to connect the Earth with the higher spirit world; as antlers are shed and regrown annually, they symbolise the magic of regeneration and renewal.

# ᐧ❋ CHARMS ❋ᐧ

> *'Now, don't forget that nice wrist movement we've been practising!'* squeaked Professor Flitwick, perched on top of his pile of books as usual. *'Swish and flick, remember, swish and flick.'*

PROFESSOR FLITWICK – HARRY POTTER AND THE PHILOSOPHER'S STONE

CHARMS ARE A WONDERFUL and important part of the wizarding world. They are spells that add different properties to objects or creatures which, as a result, often change what the object does. Students at Hogwarts learn charms for all sorts of things: a charm to cause levitation *(Wingardium Leviosa)*; a charm to open locked doors and windows *(Alohomora)*; a charm to cause confusion *(Confundo)*; a charm to tickle someone *(Rictusempra)* …

Students studying Charms must practise precise wand movements and the proper pronunciation of the incantation. A lack of concentration can lead to some unusual results.

## PROFESSOR FILIUS FLITWICK

PROFESSOR OF: CHARMS

APPEARANCE: Professor Flitwick is described as being a tiny little wizard, with a shock of white hair.

DID YOU KNOW: Professor Flitwick charms hundreds of keys as part of the protection for the Philosopher's Stone in Harry's first year at Hogwarts.

## FACT

### MAGIC WORDS

The 'magic word' is essential for a charm to work. What is thought to be the right word to make a spell work can differ all over the world. In the *1001 Arabian Nights* story, Ali Baba says *Open Sesame* to get to the robbers' treasure, while stage magicians sometimes say *Alakazam*, *Hey Presto* or *Hocus Pocus*.

> *'And saying the magic words properly is very important, too – never forget Wizard Baruffio, who said "s" instead of "f" and found himself on the floor with a buffalo on his chest.'*

PROFESSOR FLITWICK – HARRY POTTER AND THE PHILOSOPHER'S STONE

# ABRACADABRA

*'You've forgotten the magic word,' said Harry irritably. The effect of this simple sentence on the rest of the family was incredible: Dudley gasped and fell off his chair with a crash that shook the whole kitchen; Mrs Dursley gave a small scream and clapped her hands to her mouth; Mr Dursley jumped to his feet, veins throbbing in his temples.*

HARRY POTTER AND THE CHAMBER OF SECRETS

The incantation 'Abracadabra' has long been used by magicians as they perform their various tricks. In ancient times, however, the same word was believed to be a charm with healing powers. Its first ever documented use is in the *Liber Medicinalis* ('Book of Medicine') written by Quintus Serenus Sammonicus, where it was prescribed as a cure for malaria.

Sufferers were instructed to write out the word repeatedly, but each time leaving out one character. This would produce a cone-shaped text, which was then outlined in red ink. The incantation was worn as an amulet around the neck, in order to drive out the fever.

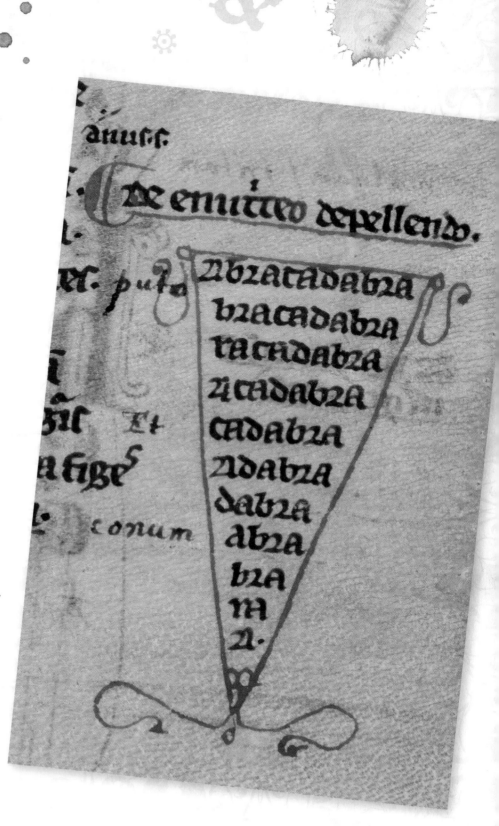

*Liber Medicinalis (Canterbury, 13th century)*
BRITISH LIBRARY

# DECIDING ON A SORTING HAT

J.K. ROWLING SPENT five years
planning Harry's world and his story.
She always knew there would be four
school houses, Gryffindor, Ravenclaw,
Hufflepuff and Slytherin, with distinct
qualities attributed to each house. But
how would the students be sorted in to
these houses?

*'Finally, I wrote a list of the ways
in which people can be chosen: eeny
meeny miny mo, short straws, chosen
by team captains, names out of a
hat – names out of a talking hat –
putting on a hat – the Sorting Hat.'*

J.K. ROWLING ON POTTERMORE

In this handwritten note,
J.K. Rowling lists different ways
the students could be sorted
into one of the four houses.
'Statues' represents her idea that
the four statues of the founders
of Hogwarts might come alive
and select students to join their
houses. Other ideas included a
ghost court, a riddle, or prefects
choosing students. Below the list
you can see her sketches of the
charmed hat of Godric Gryffindor,
complete with a mouth.

# THE SORTING HAT'S SONG

*… noticing that everyone in the Hall was now staring at the hat, he stared at it too. For a few seconds, there was complete silence. Then the hat twitched. A rip near the brim opened wide like a mouth — and the hat began to sing …*

<small>HARRY POTTER AND THE PHILOSOPHER'S STONE</small>

This is J.K. Rowling's original, handwritten draft of the Sorting Hat's song, performed in Harry's first year at the sorting ceremony. It contains some crossings-out and added edits, but most of these lines survived in the final published text of *The Philosopher's Stone*.

Oh, you may not think I'm pretty
But don't judge on what you see
I'll eat myself if you can find
A smarter hat than me
You can keep your bowlers black
Your top hats sleek and tall
For I'm the Hogwarts Sorting Hat
And I can cap them all
~~None can tell you but~~
There's nothing hidden in your ~~head~~
The Sorting Hat can't see
So try me on and I will tell ~~you~~ you
Where you ought to be.
You might belong in Gryffindor
Where dwell the brave at heart
~~It's daring, nerve and chivalry~~
~~Or Huffle~~ Their ~~If you have nor~~
~~For~~ daring, nerve and chivalry
Set Gryffindors apart
You ~~could be born for~~ might belong in Hufflepuff
~~who~~ Where ~~all are far~~ they are just and loyal
The patient
~~That patient~~ Hufflepuffs are true
And unafraid of toil
~~You may Or Ravenclaw could be your ho~~
~~The house for~~
You might belong in Ravenclaw
Where ~~the quickest~~ all quick wits are ~~prized~~ found
The ~~sharpest minds~~ wisest and most learned minds

If you've a ready mind
For Gryffindor ...
For those of wit and learning
Ravenclaw's true
And ...

*The Sorting Hat Song by J.K. Rowling*

<small>J.K. ROWLING</small>

<small>CHARMS / 51</small>

# THE OPENING TO DIAGON ALLEY

*The brick he had touched quivered – it wriggled – in the middle, a small hole appeared – it grew wider and wider – a second later they were facing an archway large enough even for Hagrid, an archway on to a cobbled street which twisted and turned out of sight.*

HARRY POTTER AND THE PHILOSOPHER'S STONE

THIS HAND-DRAWN IMAGE by J.K. Rowling shows in stages how the charmed entrance to Diagon Alley appears. Beginning with a brick wall and a dustbin, it shows the exact spot that must be tapped with a wand (in this case Hagrid's wand hidden inside an umbrella) to open the arch. The bricks begin to shift, and an opening appears, gradually getting larger until the entrance is revealed.

*Drawing of the opening to Diagon Alley by J.K. Rowling (1990)*

J.K. ROWLING

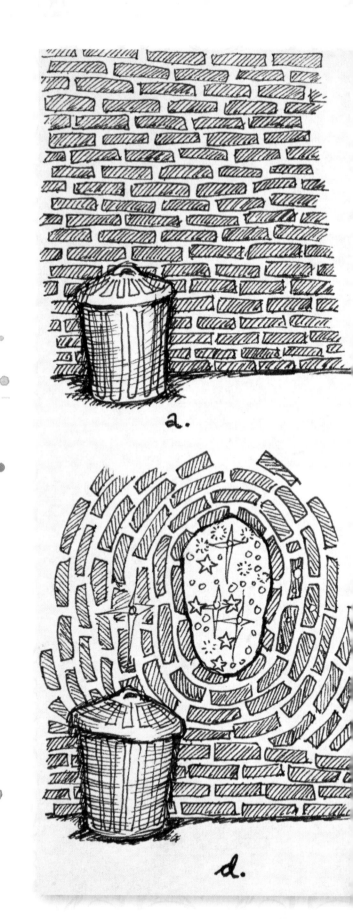

a.

d.

b.

c.

e.

f.

# A PANORAMA OF DIAGON ALLEY

JIM KAY'S INCREDIBLY detailed artwork shows the
enchanting, magical shops that make up Diagon Alley.
Kay used clever names for the shops. The telescope shop,
'Twinkles Telescopes', was inspired by a theatrical store
called Sally Twinkles he used to visit as a child, while
'*Bufo*' is the Latin genus name for toads.

*Drawing of Diagon Alley by Jim Kay*
BLOOMSBURY

There were shops selling robes, shops selling telescopes and strange silver instruments Harry had never seen before, windows stacked with barrels of bat spleens and eels' eyes, tottering piles of spell books, quills and rolls of parchment, potion bottles, globes of the moon...

HARRY POTTER AND THE PHILOSOPHER'S STONE

# Argus Filch

Argus Filch, the caretaker at Hogwarts, often came close to discovering Harry Potter on his night-time adventures around the school.

---

*Filch was the Hogwarts caretaker, a bad-tempered, failed wizard who waged a constant war against the students…*

Harry Potter and the Prisoner of Azkaban

---

This hand-drawn sketch by J.K. Rowling shows Filch holding a lamp, which might help him spot any students wandering the castle when they should be in bed.

Because Filch is a Squib (a non-magical person born to magical parents) he's unable to do any charms himself.

### Kwikspell

*Because of his inability to perform magic, Argus Filch tries to improve his skills by doing a Kwikspell Correspondence Course in Beginner's Magic. Harry Potter discovers the envelope containing information on the course during his second year at Hogwarts, much to Filch's annoyance.*

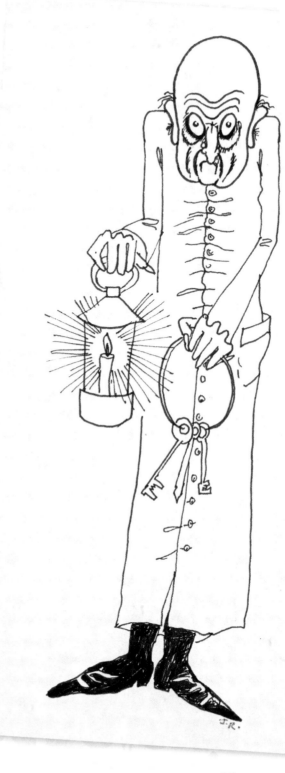

*Sketch of Argus Filch by J.K. Rowling (1990)*
J.K. ROWLING

… *Argus Filch burst suddenly through a tapestry to Harry's right, wheezing and looking wildly about for the rule-breaker.* Harry Potter and the Chamber of Secrets

# MAKE ME TO BE INVYSIBLE

'How experiments to be invisible must be prepared', in *The Book of King Solomon called The Key of Knowledge* (England, 17th century)
BRITISH LIBRARY

Invisibility cloaks are rare and valuable objects and so other ways of becoming invisible must be found. According to this chapter from *The Key of Knowledge*, entitled 'Howe experyments to be invysible must bee preparedd', one method is to recite the following charm:

'Stabbon, Asen, Gabellum, Saneney, Noty, Enobal, Labonerem, Balametem, Balnon, Tygumel, Millegaly, Juneneis, Hearma, Hamorache, Yesa, Seya, Senoy, Henen, Barucatha, Acararas, Taracub, Bucarat, Caramy, by the mercy whitch you beare towardes mann kynde, make me to be invysible.'

Several versions of this invisibility charm exist, because it was widely shared, copied and recopied. But be warned – care should be taken when reciting this spell, since nowhere does it record how to make yourself reappear!

## ACTIVITY

### BANANA MAGIC

This trick will make it seem as if you've charmed a banana inside its very own skin!

You will need a banana and a long sewing needle. Get an adult to help you push the needle through the skin of the banana and carefully move it from side to side. By doing this you will slice the banana flesh without breaking the skin. Repeat this at intervals along the banana to get several slices.

When you have finished, give the prepared banana to an unsuspecting friend. Before they open it, wave your hands above the banana and perform your favourite magic words! When they peel away the skin they will find you have already sliced the banana as if by magic …

### MAGICAL FRUIT

*In their fourth year at Hogwarts, Harry, Ron and Hermione discover how to get into the kitchens at Hogwarts from Fred and George Weasley. The door to the kitchens is concealed behind a large painting of a bowl of fruit. To get inside, all you need to do is tickle the pear in the bowl, which will squirm and chuckle before turning into a large green door handle!*

# OLGA HUNT'S BROOMSTICK

THE MOST COMMON IMAGE of a witch is one where they are flying through the night sky on a broomstick.

---

*No Muggle illustration of a witch is complete without a broom and however ludicrous these drawings are (for none of the broomsticks depicted by Muggles could stay up in the air for a moment), they remind us that we were careless for too many centuries to be surprised that broomsticks and magic are inextricably linked in the Muggle mind.* QUIDDITCH THROUGH THE AGES

---

*Broomstick belonging to Olga Hunt (England, 20th century)*
THE MUSEUM OF WITCHCRAFT AND MAGIC

The connection between witchcraft and broomsticks emerged in the 15th century. Harry and his fellow Quidditch teammates use modern and sleek brooms. This older and more traditional example was owned by a real-life woman called Olga Hunt of Manaton (Devon). During a full moon Olga would use this broomstick for magical purposes, leaping around Haytor Rocks on Dartmoor, much to the alarm of anyone in the area!

# WINGED KEYS

It's not just brooms that can fly in the wizarding world. These magically charmed keys were one of the protections put in place by the Hogwarts teachers to protect the Philosopher's Stone. The winged keys illustrations were created by digitally overlaying watercolour paintings on top of detailed pencil sketches. The artist, Jim Kay, experimented with the design and colours of the winged keys, capturing the 'whirl of rainbow feathers' described in *The Philosopher's Stone*. Each key is individually designed and beautifully detailed.

---

*'These birds … they can't be here just for decoration,' said Hermione. They watched the birds soaring overhead, glittering – glittering? 'They're not birds!' Harry said suddenly, 'they're keys! Winged keys – look carefully.'*

HARRY POTTER AND THE PHILOSOPHER'S STONE

---

Preparatory and final artwork
of winged keys by Jim Kay

BLOOMSBURY

# HARRY AND DRACO FLYING

*He mounted the broom and kicked hard against the ground and up, up he soared, air rushed through his hair and his robes whipped out behind him — and in a rush of fierce joy he realised he'd found something he could do without being taught — this was easy, this was* wonderful.

HARRY POTTER AND THE PHILOSOPHER'S STONE

THE WORLD OF MAGIC was new and complicated for Harry when he arrived at Hogwarts, but in his very first flying lesson, having never previously touched a broom, he flew so naturally that Professor McGonagall instantly whisked him away to meet the Gryffindor Quidditch team captain.

In this painting by Jim Kay, Harry is shown squinting through the rain, his hands firmly clasped around his broomstick, while Draco Malfoy heads towards him in the background.

*Harry Potter and Draco Malfoy playing Quidditch by Jim Kay*

BLOOMSBURY

# ★ ASTRONOMY ★

*They had to study the night skies through their telescopes every Wednesday at midnight and learn the names of different stars and the movements of the planets.* HARRY POTTER AND THE PHILOSOPHER'S STONE

ASTRONOMY IS ONE of the oldest sciences known to man. It is the study of the night sky and everything it contains – from stars to planets, comets, galaxies and more. Astronomy is a core subject studied at Hogwarts School of Witchcraft and Wizardry. It is also a theme in the naming of many characters. This means you can actually see the stars that are linked to the likes of Bellatrix Lestrange and Sirius Black in the night sky.

## FACT

### WHAT IS AN ASTRONOMER?

An astronomer is someone who studies the night sky and everything in it. These scientists use complicated maths to predict the movements and locations of the stars and planets. They often use high-tech telescopes and advanced digital cameras to observe the objects in the skies above us. But you don't always need fancy equipment to help you spot the stars above. Look up – what can you see?

*He flung back his head and stared at the sky. 'Mars is bright tonight.'*

RONAN ~ HARRY POTTER AND THE PHILOSOPHER'S STONE

## PROFESSOR AURORA SINISTRA

### PROFESSOR OF: ASTRONOMY

APPEARANCE: Not much is known about Professor Sinistra. She first appears in *Harry Potter and the Chamber of Secrets* but is never described in great detail. Instead her character remains somewhat of a mystery.

DID YOU KNOW: Professor Sinistra helped carry Justin Finch-Fletchley to the hospital wing after he and Nearly Headless Nick were found petrified in a deserted corridor.

Below is a small selection of characters from the Harry Potter series who share their names with the amazing stars and planets that fill our skies.

ANDROMEDA TONKS: The Andromeda galaxy takes its name from a mythological princess. Andromeda was sacrificed to a terrible sea monster but was saved by Perseus, the great monster slayer, just in time.

BELLATRIX LESTRANGE: Bellatrix (which is Latin for 'female warrior') is the third brightest star in the constellation of Orion.

REMUS LUPIN: Lupus is the wolf constellation in our night sky and Remus is a moon, which lies on an asteroid belt.

# LISTS OF HOGWARTS SUBJECTS AND TEACHERS

In this handwritten note, J.K. Rowling has listed the subjects taught at Hogwarts along with potential names of teachers. An early version of Professor Aurora Sinistra's name is recorded here as 'Aurelia Sinistra'. Latin can often be spotted in J.K. Rowling's work, especially for names and spells; 'Aurora' is Latin for 'the dawn', while 'Sinistra' is Latin for 'left-hand side'.

Enid Pettigrew

Quirinus Quirrell (1)
Gilderoy Lockhart (2) out (6),
Remus Lupin (3), (7)            Sinistra
Enid Pettigrew (4), (6), (7)
Oakden Hernshaw (5)

SUBJECTS 3'd year

core subjects
{ Potions
Transfiguration
Charms
Defence Against the Dark Arts
History of Magic
Astronomy
Herbology }

Divination ——————→ Harry & Ron
Study of Ancient Runes —→ Hermione
Arithmancy ——————→ Hermione
Care of Magical Creatures → Harry & Ron
Muggle Studies ——————→ Hermione

Divination : Enid Pettigrew

Transfiguration          Professor Minerva McGonagall
Charms                   Filius Flitwick
Potions                  Severus Snape
Defence Against the Dark Arts   Remus Lupin
History of Magic         Cuthbert Binns
Astronomy                Aurelia Sinistra
Herbology                Pomona Sprout
Divination               1
Care of Magical Creatures

---

Transfiguration     ♀     Prof. Minerva McGonagall
Charms              ♂     Prof. Filius Flitwick
Potions             ♂     Prof. Severus Snape
Herbology           ♀     Prof. Pomona Sprout
D.A.D.A.            ♀     Prof. Remus Lupin
Astronomy           ♀     Prof. Aurora Sinistra
History of Magic    ♂     Prof. Cuthbert Binns
Divination          ♀     Prof. Mopsus etc
Study of Ancient Runes  ♀  Prof. Bathsheda Babbling
Arithmancy          ♀     Prof. Septima Vector
Care of Magical Creatures ♂♂ → Rubeus Hagrid
Muggle Studies            Prof.

Digit
Pi
Vector

Septima
Vector              Hippogriffs    Stormswift
                                    Flothoof
                                    Fleetwing
Fata
The fates           Gibberish
re-hires            (Gobbledegook also check languages Greek etc
                     dogs will languages)

                    Mylor Silvanus

                    Rosmerta  "good purveyor"
                        village woman?

                    1) Quirrell
                    2) Lockhart
                    3) Lupin
                    4) Pettigrew
                    5) Mylor perm. Oakden Hobday

*Handwritten notes of subjects and teachers by J.K. Rowling*

J.K. ROWLING

# SIRIUS BLACK

THE BRIGHTEST STAR we can see from Earth is Sirius. And astronomers have been gazing at it for years on end…

As an Animagus, Sirius Black takes the form of a shaggy black dog, as does the constellation Canis Major. This medieval manuscript was made in England an astounding 900 years ago. It shows the constellation of Canis Major (which is Latin for 'the Greater Dog'), of which Sirius, the brightest star we can see from Earth, is a part. The shape of the dog in this manuscript is filled with a poem, taken from the work of a Roman author, Hyginus (died AD 17).

*Sirius (or Syrius), in Cicero's Aratea with excerpts from Hyginus, Astronomica*
BRITISH LIBRARY

## ACTIVITY

### *HOW TO FIND SIRIUS*

Wait for a dark and clear night to try this. To find Sirius, you need to use Orion's Belt as a guide. The three stars which make up Orion's Belt point down to Sirius, which sits beneath them, to the left. It should be easy to recognise as it's our sky's brightest star.

ORION

Orion's Belt

Sirius

... *Harry saw something that distracted him completely: the silhouette of an enormous shaggy black dog, clearly imprinted against the sky, motionless in the topmost, empty row of seats.*

HARRY POTTER AND THE PRISONER OF AZKABAN

*Sirius Black in his Animagus form by Jim Kay*

BLOOMSBURY

# AN ANGLO-SAXON CENTAUR

*And into the clearing came –
was it a man, or a horse?
To the waist, a man, with red
hair and beard, but below that
was a horse's gleaming chestnut
body with a long, reddish tail.*

HARRY POTTER AND THE PHILOSOPHER'S STONE

## FACT

Stars and constellations all have
different and unique names – usually with an
interesting story or meaning behind them.
Here is a selection of some of the wonderful
animal constellations that fill our skies.

APUS – THE BIRD OF PARADISE
AQUILA – THE EAGLE
ARIES – THE RAM
CAMELOPARDALIS – THE GIRAFFE
CANCER – THE CRAB
CANES VENATICI – THE HUNTING DOGS
CAPRICORNUS – THE SEA GOAT

*Capricorn, in Cicero's Aratea*
BRITISH LIBRARY

THE CONSTELLATION SAGITTARIUS is usually depicted
as a centaur and its name comes from the Latin word for
'archer'. The Sagittarius constellation is illustrated in this
Anglo-Saxon manuscript as a centaur (a half-human and
half-horse mythological creature) made shortly before
England was invaded by the Normans in 1066. The arrow
is aimed at Capricorn on the opposite page; the stars are
represented by orange-red orbs. When joined together,
the goat and centaur take shape.

J.K. Rowling's centaurs first appear in *Harry Potter and the
Philosopher's Stone*. Harry meets Ronan and Bane, who
read what is to come in the movements of the planets.
In *Harry Potter and the Order of the Phoenix*, the centaur
Firenze becomes a teacher of Divination at Hogwarts.

Orange-red orbs represent stars

*Sagittarius, in Cicero's Aratea*
BRITISH LIBRARY

# CENTAURS

Centaurs originate from Greek mythology and combine
the strength of a horse with the intelligence of a human.

*'Never,' said Hagrid irritably,
'try an' get a straight answer
out of a centaur. Ruddy
star-gazers. Not interested in
anythin' closer'n the moon.'*

HARRY POTTER AND THE PHILOSOPHER'S STONE

Throughout history different explanations have been
offered for how these creatures came to exist. Some say
that they are the result of a union between a giant and
a horse, while others believe that these creatures were
once a group of giants called the Titans. The giants
entered into battle with the gods but were defeated and
given the lower bodies of a horse as punishment.

# AN ARABIC ASTROLABE

BEFORE COMPUTERS and the digital age, astronomers used other means to help them observe and chart the objects in the night sky.

In the list of things needed for new Hogwarts students, alongside books, a wand, a cauldron, and more, was one telescope. Harry Potter bought his collapsible brass telescope in Diagon Alley.

Keen students may have looked past the set equipment list and bought more intricate equipment such as an astrolabe.

Arabic numerals embedded in silver

An astrolabe found in Syria (13th century)
BRITISH MUSEUM

*Other Equipment*
*1 wand*
*1 cauldron (pewter, standard size 2)*
*1 set glass or crystal phials*
*1 telescope*
*1 set brass scales*

HARRY POTTER AND THE PHILOSOPHER'S STONE

Invented by the Greeks, astrolabes provided a two-dimensional map of the heavens. They could be used to identify the stars and planets (always helpful for drawing up a star chart) and for determining latitude.

They were also used to find the direction of Mecca, which Muslims face when they pray. This finely decorated example is made of brass inlaid with silver.

'Welcome,' said Hagrid, 'to Diagon Alley.'
HARRY POTTER AND THE PHILOSOPHER'S STONE

# Urania's Mirror

Any stargazer would benefit from getting their hands on *Urania's Mirror; or, a View of the Heavens* – a set of 32 cards charting the night's sky.

Each card is pierced with little holes that relate to the size of the brightest stars in the sky. When held up to the light this gives the viewer a realistic impression of what each constellation might look like.

*Urania's Mirror: Box interior (London, 1834)*
BRITISH LIBRARY

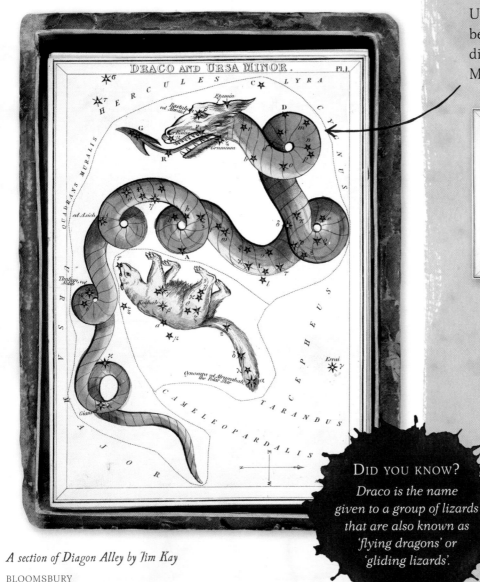

*A section of Diagon Alley by Jim Kay*
BLOOMSBURY

*When they reached the top of the Astronomy Tower at eleven o'clock, they found a perfect night for stargazing, cloudless and still.*

HARRY POTTER AND THE ORDER OF THE PHOENIX

The two constellations shown here are Draco and Ursa Minor, represented by a dragon and a little bear. Draco, one of the earliest constellations to be discovered, lends its name to Harry's nemesis, Draco Malfoy. In Latin it means 'dragon'.

*Urania's Mirror: Cards of the constellations*
BRITISH LIBRARY

**DID YOU KNOW?**
*Draco is the name given to a group of lizards that are also known as 'flying dragons' or 'gliding lizards'.*

# THE LATITUDE OF THE MOON

PETRUS APIANUS (1495–1522), the son of a shoemaker, was a brilliant German astronomer, mathematician and printer. He created a beautiful book, which contains a series of rotating paper models, known as volvelles. The movement of the discs pinned at their centre mimics the movement of the planets.

This example shows the reader how to find the latitude of the moon. A dragon (with a head that looks like a rat) sits in the middle, and can be spun round to point at different zodiac signs, which are included on the edge of the circle. The volvelles could be used in turn to write horoscopes, showing that the distinction between astrology and astronomy was rather blurred in the 16th century.

Zodiac signs

## FACT

### *WHAT IS ASTROLOGY?*

Astrology is the study of the movements and positions of natural objects visible in the night sky. Some people believe that these objects have an effect on events on Earth and on human behaviour.

*Astronomicum Caesareum (Ingolstadt, 1540)*
BRITISH LIBRARY

### DID YOU KNOW?
*A zodiac is the area of the sky occupied by the sun at the moment of your birth. There are 12 different signs, each of which is associated with a different month – Aries, Taurus, Gemini, Cancer, Leo, Virgo, Libra, Scorpio, Sagittarius, Capricorn, Aquarius and Pisces.*

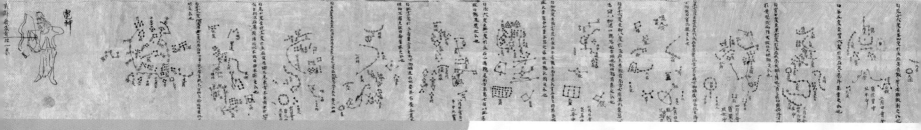

# THE OLDEST ATLAS OF THE NIGHT SKY

This piece of paper is the oldest complete preserved star atlas from any civilisation. Discovered in China by Aurel Stein in 1907, it shows more than 1,300 stars visible to the naked eye in the Northern Hemisphere, centuries before the invention of the telescope.

---

*'I know that you have learned the names of the planets and their moons in Astronomy,' said Firenze's calm voice, 'and that you have mapped the stars' progress through the heavens.'*

HARRY POTTER AND THE ORDER OF THE PHOENIX

---

In China, around the time that the atlas was made (AD 700), it was believed that the movement of the stars directly reflected the actions of the emperor and the court on Earth. A solar eclipse, for example, might have been a sign that an invasion was coming. The three different colours, black, red and white, included in the atlas represent the stars identified by ancient Chinese astronomers, working over a thousand years before this atlas was made.

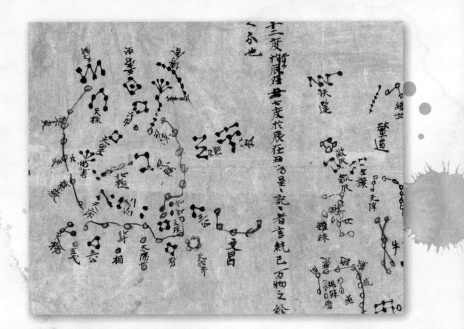

*The Dunhuang star chart, the earliest known manuscript atlas of the night sky (China, c. 700)*

BRITISH LIBRARY

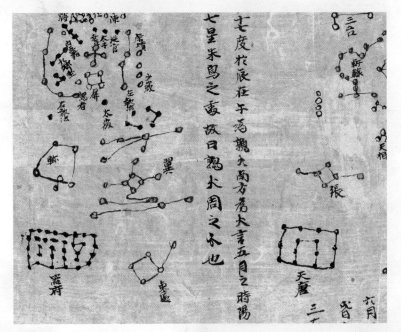

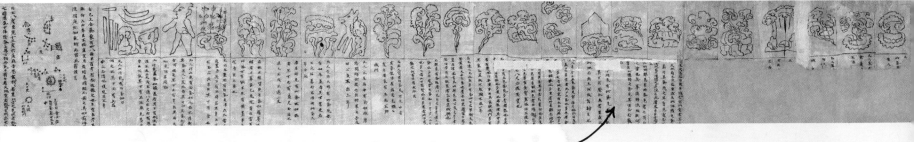

*The ancient atlas is 2 metres in length*

# LEONARDO DA VINCI ON THE MOON

LEONARDO DA VINCI, inventor, scientist, artist, was centuries ahead of his time. Throughout his career, Leonardo wrote countless notes in mirror handwriting (reading from right to left). The shaded diagram in the centre right of the image below describes the reflection of light, according to the alignments of the Sun, Moon and Earth.

Leonardo also believed that the Moon was covered with water, and that its surface would operate like a convex mirror, reflecting light.

*Astronomical notes and sketches, in Leonardo da Vinci's notebook (Italy, 16th century)*

BRITISH LIBRARY

**DID YOU KNOW?**
*Planet Earth is not the only planet in our solar system that has its own moon. Jupiter has 67 known moons!*

'The happiest man on earth would be able to use the Mirror of Erised like a normal mirror, that is, he would look into it and see himself exactly as he is ... It shows us nothing more or less than the deepest, most desperate desire of our hearts.'

PROFESSOR DUMBLEDORE – HARRY POTTER AND THE PHILOSOPHER'S STONE

## ACTIVITY

### SECRET WRITING

The following inscription is carved on the Mirror of Erised, which Harry discovers in *Harry Potter and the Philosopher's Stone*. Copy out the line on to a separate piece of paper. Start with the last letter of the inscription to begin. Then work backwards to uncover what the inscription says.

*Erised stra ehru oyt ube cafru oyt on wohsi.*

HARRY POTTER AND THE PHILOSOPHER'S STONE

ANSWER: I show not your face but your heart's desire

# DIVINATION

*'So you have chosen to study Divination, the most difficult of all magical arts. I must warn you at the outset that if you do not have the Sight, there is very little I will be able to teach you ...'*

PROFESSOR TRELAWNEY – HARRY POTTER AND THE PRISONER OF AZKABAN

INDIVIDUALS PRACTISING Divination seek knowledge about the future and the unknown. The art of Divination has been practised for years on end, by countless different cultures and in many ways; palmistry, crystal balls, cards, and tea leaves are just a few of the methods that seers use to look into the future to make their predictions.

## PROPHECIES

*Genuine prophecies made by Professor Trelawney were kept inside glass balls in the Department of Mysteries, a top-secret place inside the Ministry of Magic. Only those about whom a prophecy is made are able to retrieve it.*

*Portrait of Professor Sybill Trelawney by Jim Kay*

BLOOMSBURY

## PROFESSOR SYBILL TRELAWNEY

### PROFESSOR OF: DIVINATION

APPEARANCE: Professor Trelawney is very thin with large glasses that magnify her eyes to several times their natural size. She is described as wearing a shawl, with many chains and beads around her neck and countless bangles and rings on her arms and hands.

DID YOU KNOW: Professor Trelawney was the great-great-granddaughter of the celebrated Seer Cassandra Trelawney. A seer, also known as a diviner, is someone who is supposed to be able to look into the future and predict what is to come. Both names, 'Sybill' and 'Cassandra', relate to the word 'seer'. Throughout history the word 'sibyl' has been used to refer to any woman who can look into the future, while Cassandra was a Trojan seer who received the gift of prophecy from Apollo.

## FACT

### PREDICTING THE FUTURE

For thousands of years people have tried to find out what their futures might hold. Some of the more unusual methods involve interpreting cloud formations, the flight of birds, or the entrails (guts) or liver of sacrificed animals. There is even a method called moleosophy which looks at moles and birthmarks to predict the future.

# Mother Shipton

This book, published in 1797, talks about the Yorkshire prophetess, Mother Shipton. No one knows for sure if she existed and very little is known about her life, but apparently she had a long, rounded nose and a protruding hairy chin, and together with her powers to predict the future, legend has it that she was also able to levitate.

She made her most famous prophecy in 1530. She predicted that Cardinal Wolsey, who had been made Archbishop of York, would see the city of York but never reach it. According to the book from which this image is taken, Wolsey saw the city from the top of a nearby castle, but was immediately arrested and taken to London, and so, as Mother Shipton predicted, he never actually reached the city.

Today, Mother Shipton is best known for her birthplace, which was supposedly near the 'Dropping Well' in Knaresborough, Yorkshire. Long believed to have magical properties, the waters of the well were said to turn objects to stone within a few weeks.

### Did you know?

*The Dropping Well doesn't really turn things to stone. However, the water contains lots of minerals. If the water drips over an object for long enough, the water gradually evaporates and the minerals are left behind. This forms a crusty coating that looks like stone.*

*Wonders!!! Past, Present, and to come; being the strange prophecies and uncommon predictions of the famous Mother Shipton (London, 1797)*
BRITISH LIBRARY

THE FAMOUS MOTHER SHIPTON

*Published as the Act directs by Samuel Baker. Aug.t 1. 1797*

# A WITCH'S SCRYING MIRROR

Using a mirror or another reflective surface to predict the future is an ancient practice known as 'scrying'. The term originates from the word 'descry', which means 'to catch sight of'. The practice involves looking into a shiny surface in the hope of detecting some form of message or vision.

This item once belonged to the witch Cecil Williamson (1909–1999). Williamson warned if you gaze into it: 'and suddenly see someone standing behind you, whatever you do, do not turn around'.

Although the Mirror of Erised, which Harry discovers in *Harry Potter and the Philosopher's Stone*, is also a mirror, it is not used for scrying. Instead, it reveals to the person looking into it their deepest desires.

*'It does not do to dwell on dreams and forget to live, remember that.'*

PROFESSOR DUMBLEDORE – HARRY POTTER AND THE PHILOSOPHER'S STONE

*A wooden witch mirror*

THE MUSEUM OF WITCHCRAFT AND MAGIC

# CRYSTAL BALLS

*'Crystal-gazing is a particularly refined art,' she said dreamily. 'I do not expect any of you to See when first you peer into the Orb's infinite depths. We shall start by practising relaxing the conscious mind and external eyes ... so as to clear the Inner Eye and the superconscious. Perhaps, if we are lucky, some of you will See before the end of the class.'*

PROFESSOR TRELAWNEY – HARRY POTTER AND THE PRISONER OF AZKABAN

CRYSTALLOMANCY – to give it its technical term – has its roots in the Middle Ages, with crystal balls remaining one of the best known divination tools.

This large crystal ball is typical of the orbs used in the 20th century; it has an elaborate stand made up of three griffins at the base of an Egyptian-style column.

*A crystal ball and stand*
THE MUSEUM OF WITCHCRAFT AND MAGIC

*It was stiflingly warm, and the fire which was burning under the crowded mantelpiece was giving off a heavy, sickly sort of perfume as it heated a large copper kettle.*

The witch 'Smelly Nelly', who used the black crystal ball below, had a taste for strong perfume; she believed that the smell appealed to the spirits who helped her to predict the future. Known as a moon crystal, the black ball was used at night, so that the seer could read the moon's reflection in it. One witness who saw Smelly Nelly using this ball reported how, 'You caught her scent a mile off downwind'; to be out with a 'full moon, Smelly Nelly and her crystal [was] quite an experience.'

*A black moon crystal ball*
THE MUSEUM OF
WITCHCRAFT AND MAGIC

# CHINESE ORACLE BONES

Oracle bones were used for an ancient Chinese divination ritual over three thousand years ago. Questions about war, agriculture and natural disasters were engraved on the bones. Heat was then applied to the bones with metal sticks, causing them to crack. The diviners would interpret the patterns of the cracks to find the answers to the questions posed.

The bone below is carved with the Shang Dynasty script, the oldest known form of Chinese writing. The inscription on this shoulder bone says that there will be no misfortune in the coming ten days. The character for 'moon' (*yue* in modern Chinese) is visible at the top of the bone in the centre. On the reverse of the bone is a record of a lunar eclipse that experts have dated to 27th December 1192 BC: the darkness caused by an eclipse was considered to be a bad omen, indicating that an ancestral spirit needed to be pacified.

DID YOU KNOW?

*Chinese oracle bones were often made from an ox's shoulder blade (scapula), or from the flat underside of a turtle shell (the plastron).*

*Oracle bone (China, 1192 BC)*
BRITISH LIBRARY

# A Thai Divination Manual

In 19th-century Siam (modern-day Thailand), people consulted a divination specialist, known as a *mor doo*, on matters of love and relationships. This divination manual, or *phrommachat*, contains horoscopes based on the Chinese zodiac, including drawings of the 12 zodiac animals and their attributes (earth, wood, fire, iron, water).

Each zodiac page is followed by a series of paintings, which symbolise the fate of a person under certain circumstances. The unnamed artist paid great attention to every single detail in the illustrations – facial expression, hand gestures, body language, and the elaborate designs of their clothes and jewellery. Most interestingly, the manuscript describes lucky and unlucky constellations for couples, taking into consideration their characters as well as their horoscopes.

*A Thai divination manual –*
*phrommachat (Siam, 19th century)*
BRITISH LIBRARY

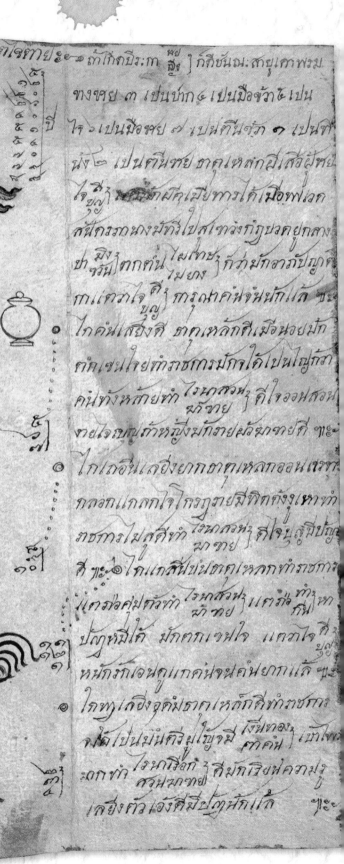

# THE CHINESE ZODIAC

The Chinese zodiac follows a 12-year cycle, with each year represented by a different animal, always in the same order. The Year of the Rat marks the start of every new 12-year cycle.

Each animal has characteristics that are supposed to affect people born during that year. For instance, people with the rooster sign are believed to be honest, ambitious and clever, while those with a monkey sign are gentle, honest and quick-witted.

Why these particular animals though? There are lots of different stories to explain this. In one particular tale a great emperor said he would name the years after the animals in the order in which they arrived at his palace.

The animals had to cross a river to get to the palace. Any animal that could swim jumped straight in. However, the rat and the cat couldn't swim and so jumped on to the ox for a free ride. But just before they reached the shore, the rat pushed the cat into the water and ran ahead to become the first. This is why there is no Year of the Cat!

## ZODIAC ANIMALS

RAT

OX

TIGER

RABBIT

DRAGON

SNAKE

HORSE

GOAT

MONKEY

ROOSTER

DOG

PIG

# Divination
# Playing Cards

... *Professor Trelawney appeared round a corner, muttering to herself as she shuffled a pack of dirty-looking playing cards, reading them as she walked. 'Two of spades: conflict,' she murmured, as she passed the place where Harry crouched, hidden. 'Seven of spades: an ill omen. Ten of spades: violence. Knave of spades: a dark young man, possibly troubled, one who dislikes the questioner –'*

HARRY POTTER AND THE HALF-BLOOD PRINCE

A pack of divination playing cards
(London, c. 1745–1756)
BRITISH MUSEUM

CARTOMANCY IS A FORM of divination that uses cards to predict the future. Although playing cards have long been used in fortune-telling, this pack is said to be the earliest designed specifically for divination. Created in the 18th century by the card specialist John Lenthall (1683–1762), the 52 cards follow an unusual procedure.

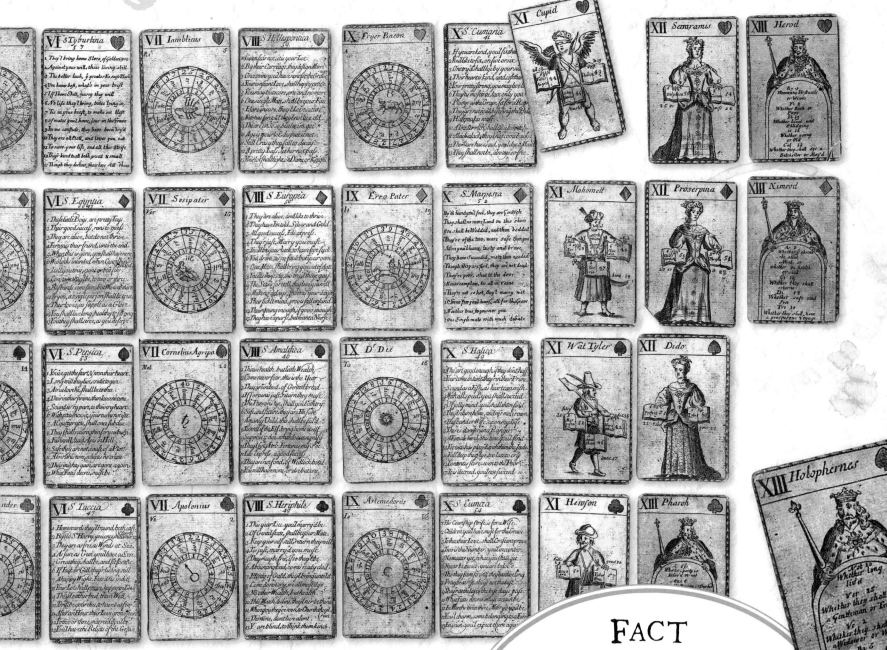

The kings in the pack prompt questions that are answered in the form of mysterious rhyming phrases. Each card was inscribed with the names of famous astronomers, seers and magicians, including Merlin, Doctor Faust and Nostradamus, in the hope that their association with astrology and divination would enhance confidence in the cards' predictions.

## FACT

❊ Merlin was the legendary magician who advised King Arthur.

❊ Doctor Faust is a character in German legend, who gave his soul to the devil in exchange for unlimited knowledge and pleasure.

❊ Nostradamus really existed – he was a French doctor who published a book of prophecies in 1555.

# PALMISTRY

*Professor Trelawney was now teaching them palmistry, and she lost no time in informing Harry that he had the shortest life-lines she had ever seen.*

<small>HARRY POTTER AND THE PRISONER OF AZKABAN</small>

PALMISTRY, ALSO KNOWN as chiromancy, is an ancient method of divination that uses the shapes and lines of the hand to predict the future. The practice first became popular in Western Europe in the 12th century, under Arabic influence.

The medieval manuscript in which this image is found contains a collection of texts on fortune-telling. Every hand contains three natural lines, forming a 'triangle'. This diagram shows a right hand, on to which is mapped the natural lines and other accidental lines. One vertical line running across the palm reads, 'This line represents love'. Another vertical line running between the middle and index finger has a less fortunate meaning: 'This line signifies a bloody death and if the line reaches unto the middle of the finger it signifies a sudden death.' Other lines are said to predict ailments and diseases, such as eye problems and the plague, and personality traits, such as courage.

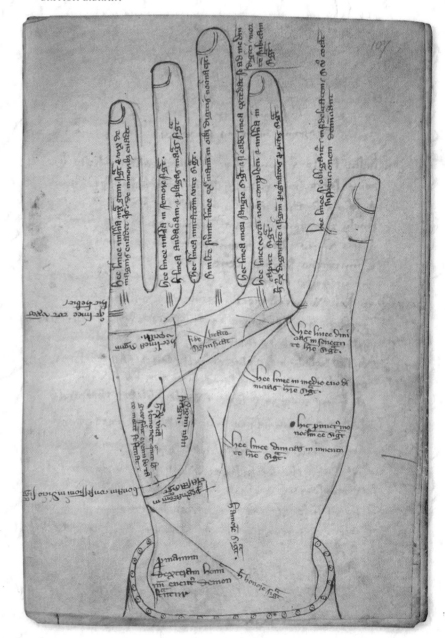

Reading the hands, in a fortune-telling manuscript (England, 14th century)

BRITISH LIBRARY

*[Harry] rounded off the whole fiasco by mixing up the life and head lines on her palm and informing her that she ought to have died the previous Tuesday.* <small>HARRY POTTER AND THE ORDER OF THE PHOENIX</small>

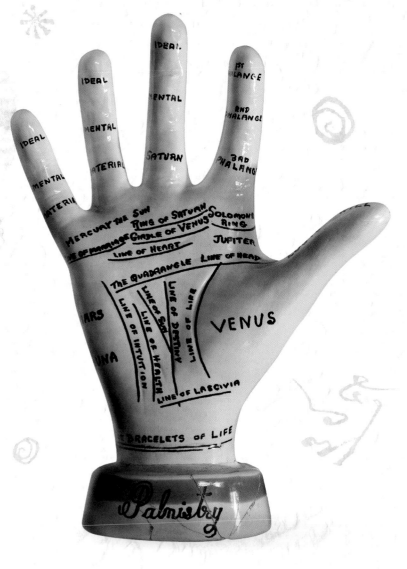

The labels on the ceramic palmistry hand include:

IDEAL · MENTAL · 1ST PHALANGE · 2ND PHALANGE · 3RD PHALANGE · MENTAL · SATURN · MATERIAL · MERCURY · THE SUN · RING OF SATURN · SOLOMONS RING · LINE OF MARS · GIRDLE OF VENUS · JUPITER · LINE OF HEART · THE QUADRANGLE · LINE OF HEAD · MARS · LINE OF LIFE · LINE OF SUN · LINE OF DESTINY · VENUS · LINE OF HEALTH · LUNA · LINE OF INTUITION · LINE OF LASCIVIA · BRACELETS OF LIFE · *Palmistry*

This ceramic palmistry hand, which would have been used for reference, shows the significant lines and mounts on the palm and wrist along with some of their meanings. Hands like this were first manufactured in Britain in the 1880s. Palmistry became increasingly popular during this time due to the work of the celebrated astrologer William John Warner (1866–1936), also known as Cheiro or Count Louis Hamon. Warner had a number of famous clients, including Oscar Wilde and the Prince of Wales, for whom he made personal predictions.

*A palmistry hand*

# ACTIVITY

Want to find the lines on your own palm? Start by making a print of your palm, like a giant fingerprint – this will make the lines easier to see. Press your palm and fingers on to an inkpad until they're nice and inky, then press firmly on to a piece of white paper and lift straight up again. Without re-inking, press again on to a second piece of paper (there is sometimes too much ink on the first attempt). You should be able to see your palm lines clearly. There are four major lines on your palm – the heart line, the head line, the life line and the fate line. Can you find them on your handprint?

1) THE HEART LINE
2) THE HEAD LINE
3) THE FATE LINE
4) THE LIFE LINE

# TEA LEAVES

Tasseography, taken from the French word *tasse*, meaning 'cup', and the Greek word *graph*, meaning 'writing', is a form of divination that uses the sediment in cups, usually left by tea leaves, to look into the future.

These pages come from a small volume on tea leaf divination, which traces the first use of tasseography to 229 BC. In that year, a Chinese princess rejected astrological predictions in favour of a new tea leaf reading technique introduced to her by a student.

The pamphlet contains a handy guide to decoding a range of shapes formed by leaves in the bottom of the cup. Some of the shapes are remarkably difficult to tell apart, such as numbers 38 and 42, which mean 'You will meet a stranger' and 'You will make an enemy'. A lot of the predictions are quite general while others are bizarrely specific, like number 44, which indicates, 'You will be interested in the Navy'!

*How to Read the Future with Tea Leaves, translated from the Chinese by Mandra (Stamford, c. 1925)*

BRITISH LIBRARY

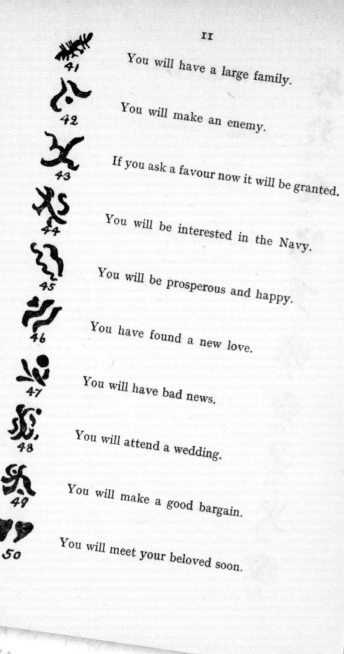

II

41 You will have a large family.

42 You will make an enemy.

43 If you ask a favour now it will be granted.

44 You will be interested in the Navy.

45 You will be prosperous and happy.

46 You have found a new love.

47 You will have bad news.

48 You will attend a wedding.

49 You will make a good bargain.

50 You will meet your beloved soon.

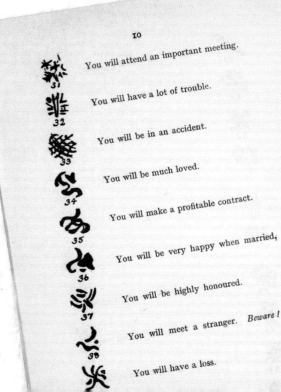

IO

31 You will attend an important meeting.

32 You will have a lot of trouble.

33 You will be in an accident.

34 You will be much loved.

35 You will make a profitable contract.

36 You will be very happy when married.

37 You will be highly honoured.

38 You will meet a stranger. *Beware!*

You will have a loss.

The first European accounts of this method of divination appeared in the 17th century, following the introduction of tea from China. The location and shape of the tea leaves in the cup symbolise different things. This pink divination cup (opposite) was made in the 1930s by Paragon, a Staffordshire manufacturer of bone china. Inside it are symbols to help interpret the leaves, along with the following quote around the rim: 'Many curious things I see when telling fortunes in your tea.'

'*Right, you've got a wonky sort of cross...*' *he said, consulting* Unfogging the Future. '*That means you're going to have "trials and suffering" — sorry about that — but there's a thing that could be the sun. Hang on ... that means "great happiness" ... so you're going to suffer but be very happy ...*'

RON – HARRY POTTER AND THE PRISONER OF AZKABAN

*A fortune-telling cup and saucer made by Paragon (Stoke-on-Trent, c. 1932–39)*

THE MUSEUM OF WITCHCRAFT AND MAGIC

# A SCOTTISH DIVINATION MANUAL

This detailed manual on tea leaf divination practised in Scotland was written by an unnamed author, described on the title page as 'a Highland Seer'. It provides instructions not only on interpreting the various shapes made by the leaves, but also on the ideal size and shape of cup, the type of tea to use, and even on the significance of where a symbol appears within the cup. For example, the author writes that the nearer an image appears to the handle of the cup, the sooner the predicted event will occur.

## DID YOU KNOW?

*Tea is made from the leaves of the camellia bush. People actually grow this in the UK for its lovely flowers.*

TEA CUP READING

HOW TO TELL FORTUNES BY TEA LEAVES

WITH EXPLANATORY ILLUSTRATIONS

BY A HIGHLAND SEER

*Tea Cup Reading: How to Tell Fortunes by Tea Leaves by a Highland Seer (Toronto, c. 1920)*

BRITISH LIBRARY

# DEFENCE AGAINST THE DARK ARTS

*The class everyone had really been looking forward to was Defence Against the Dark Arts ...*

DEFENCE AGAINST THE DARK ARTS is a compulsory subject taught at Hogwarts School of Witchcraft and Wizardry. In this class students learn how to defend themselves from the Dark Arts, Dark creatures and an array of Dark curses. Rumour has it that the position for the job was jinxed, meaning that each new school year brought with it a new Defence Against the Dark Arts teacher.

## FACT

### HISTORICAL DEFENCE

Throughout history people have attempted to protect themselves from the Dark Arts. In Britain, pentangles, flower patterns and the letters V and M (standing for the Virgin Mary) were often scratched into stones near the doors, windows and chimneys of houses in the hope that this would stop witches getting in. Rowan trees were also supposed to keep away evil spirits. The trees were planted in graveyards to watch over the spirits of the dead, and people carried little sprigs of rowan or pinned them over doorways to keep them safe.

### PROFESSOR QUIRINUS QUIRRELL
A nervous and trembling man, Professor Quirrell wore a large purple turban to hide a dark secret.

### PROFESSOR GILDEROY LOCKHART
With dazzlingly white teeth and forget-me-not blue eyes, Professor Lockhart had a wink and a smile that fooled almost everyone.

### PROFESSOR REMUS JOHN LUPIN
Many students considered Lupin to be one of the best Defence Against the Dark Arts teachers they'd ever had. Professor Lupin was bitten by Fenrir Greyback as a child and kept his werewolf secret hidden for many years.

### PROFESSOR ALASTOR MOODY (MAD-EYE MOODY)
Later revealed to be none other than Barty Crouch Jr taking the form of Professor Moody by using Polyjuice Potion.

### PROFESSOR DOLORES UMBRIDGE
Squat, broad and with a flabby face, Professor Umbridge reminded Harry of a large toad the first time he saw her.

### PROFESSOR SEVERUS SNAPE
With greasy black hair and sallow skin, Professor Snape finally fulfils his dream of becoming the Defence Against the Dark Arts teacher in Harry's sixth year at Hogwarts.

### PROFESSOR AMYCUS CARROW
Brother to Alecto, Professor Carrow took up the role of Defence Against the Dark Arts teacher in *Harry Potter and the Deathly Hallows*.

*Portrait of Professor Lupin by Jim Kay*
BLOOMSBURY

# RED EYES

In *HARRY POTTER AND THE PHILOSOPHER'S Stone*, Harry learns of the existence of Lord Voldemort, leader of the Death Eaters and master of the Dark Arts.

These typed pages are part of an early draft of *Harry Potter and the Philosopher's Stone*.

*'… the only book I typed on my old electric typewriter.'*

J.K. ROWLING, 2017

While many details of the world described in this chapter are familiar from the published books, these scenes provide a very different version of the beginning of the story. For example, Dudley is called 'Didsbury' in this early draft and Fudge is a Muggle!

This scene is reminiscent of Cornelius Fudge visiting the Prime Minister of the Muggles in the first chapter of *Harry Potter and the Half-Blood Prince*.

*'I often cut ideas and put them into later books. Never waste a good scene!'*

J.K. ROWLING, 2017

Hagrid goes to see Fudge in his office to warn him about You-Know-Who (even in this early draft Hagrid won't say the name), and in turn, Fudge warns the public about this red-eyed dwarf, as he is described. The red eyes remain in the final description of Lord Voldemort, but the character took time to develop fully into the terrifying figure we know from the published stories.

"Your kind?"

"Yeah... our kind. We're the ones who've bin disappearin'. We're all in hidin' now. But I can't tell yeh much abou' us. Can't 'ave Muggles knowin' our business. But this is gettin' outta hand, an' all you Muggles are gettin' involved - them on the train, fer instance - they shouldn'ta bin hurt like that. That's why Dumbledore sent me. Says it's your business too, now."

"You've come to tell me why all these houses are disappearing?" Fudge said, "And why all these people are being killed?"

"Ah, well now, we're not sure they 'ave bin killed," said the giant. "He's jus' taken them. Needs 'em, see. 'E's picked on the best. Dedalus Diggle, Elsie Bones, Angus an' Elspeth McKinnon ... yeah, 'e wants 'em on 'is side."

"You're talking about this little red-eyed -?"

"Shh!" hissed the giant. "Not so loud! 'E could be 'ere now, fer all we know!"

Fudge shuddered ~~shivered~~ and looked wildly aroudn them. "C - could he?"

"S'alright, I don' reckon I was followed," said the giant in a gravelly whisper.

"But who is this person? What is he? One of - um - your kind?"

The giant snorted.

"Was once, I s'pose," he said. "But I don' think 'e's anything yeh could put a name to any more. 'E's not a 'uman. ~~'E's not an animal. 'E's not properly~~ Wish 'e was. 'E could be killed if 'e was still 'uman enough."

"He can't be <u>killed</u>?" whispered Fudge in terror.

"Well, we don' think so. But Dumbledore's workin' on it. 'E's gotta be stopped, see?"

"Well, yes of course," said Fudge. "We can't have this sort of thing going on..."

"This is nothin'," said the giant, "'E's just gettin' started. Once 'e's got the power, once 'e's got the followers, no-one'll be safe. Not even Muggles. I 'eard 'e'll keep yeh alive, though. Fer slaves."

Fudge's eyes bulged with terror.

~~"But who is this - this person?~~"

"This Bumblebore - Dunderbore -"

"Albus Dumbledore," said the the giant severely.

"Yes, yes, him - you say he has a plan?"

"Oh, yeah. So it's not hopeless yet. Reckon Dumbledore's the only one "He's still afraid of. But 'e needs your 'elp. I'm 'ere teh ask yeh.

""Oh dear," said Fudge breathlessly, "The thing is, I'd be
was planning to retire early. Tomorrow, as a matter of fact. Mrs.
Fudge and I were thinking of moving to Portugal. We have a villa-"

The giant lent forward, his beetle brows low over his glinting
eyes.

"Yeh won' be safe in Portugal if 'e ain' stopped, Fudge."

"Won't I?" said Fudge weakly, "Oh, very well then... what is
it Mr. Dumblething wants?"

"Dumbledore," said the giant. "Three things. First, yeh
gotta put out a message. On television, an' radio, an' in the
newspapers. Warn people not teh give 'im directions. 'Cause
that's 'ow 'e's gettin' us, see? 'E 'as ter be told. Feeds on
betrayal. I don' blame the Muggles, mind, they didn' know what
they were doin'.

"Second, yeh gotta make sure ye're not teh tell anyone abou'
us. If Dumbledore manages ter get rid of 'im, yeh gotta swear
not ter go spreadin' it about what yeh know, abou' us. We keeps
ourselves quiet, see? Let it stay that way.

An' third, yeh gotta give me a drink before I go. I gotta
long journey back."

The giant's face creased into a grin behind his wild beard.

"Oh - yes, of course," said Fudge shakily, "Help yourself -
there's brandy up there - and - not that I suppose it will happen -
I mean, I'm a Muddle - a Muffle - no, a Muggle - but if this
person - this thing - comes looking for me -?"

"Yeh'll be dead," said the giant flatly over the top of a large
glass of brandy. "No-one can survive if 'e attacks them, 'Ain'
never been a survivor. But like yeh say, yer a Muggle. 'E's
not interested in you."

The giant drained his glass and stood up. He pulled out an
umbrealla. It was pink and had flowers on it.

"I'll be off, then," he said.

"Just one thing," said Fudge, watching curiously as the giant
opened the umbrella, "What is this - person's - name."

The giant looked suddenly scared.

"Can' tell yeh that," he said, "We never say it. Never."

He raised the pink umbrella over his head, Fudge blinked -
and the giant was gone.                    *  *  *  *  *

*An early draft of Harry Potter
and the Philosopher's Stone*

J.K. ROWLING

Fudge wondered, of course, if he was going mad.  He seriously considerd the possibility that the giant had been a hallucination.  But the brandy glass the giant had drunk from was real enough, left standing on his desk.

Fudge wouldn't let his secretary remove the glass next day.  It reassured him he wasn't a lunatic to do what he knew he had to do.  He telephoned all the journalists he knew, and all the television stations, chose his favourite tie and gave a press conference.  He told the world there was a ~~maniac~~ madman ~~about~~ a strange little man going about.  A little man with red eyes. he told the public to be very careful not to tell this little man where anyone lived.  Once he had given out this strange message, he said "Any questions?"  But the room was completely silent.  Clearly, they all thought he was off his rocker.  Fudge went back to his office and sat staring at the giant's empty brandy glass.  ~~This was the end of his career.~~

The very last person he wanted to see was Vernone Dursley.  Dursley woudl be delighted.  Dursley would be happily counting the days until he was made Minister, now that Fudge was so clearly nuttier than a bag of salted peanuts.

But Fudge had another surprise in store.  Dursley knocked quietly, came into his office, sat opposite him and said flatly,

You've had a visit from One of Them, haven't you?"

"~~One of~~  Fudge looked at Dursley in amazement.

"You - know?"

"Yes," said Dursley bitterly, "I've known from the start.  Of course, I - happened to know there were people like that.  Of course, I never told anyone.

                    *    *    *    *    *


~~Most peep-~~
Perhaps ~~people did-~~ most people did think Fudge

Whether or not nearly everyone thought Fudge had gone very strange, the fact was that he seemed to have stopped the odd accidents.  Three whole weeks passed, and still the empty brandy glass stood on Fudge's desk to give him courage, and not one bus flew, the houses of Britain stayed where they were, the trains stopped going swimming.  Fudge, who hadn't even told Mrs. Fudge about the giant with the pink umbrella, waited and prayed and slept with his fingers crossed.  Surely this Dumbledore would send a message if they'd managed to get rid of the red eyed dwarf?  Or did this horrible silence mean that the dwarf had in fact got everyone he wanted, that he was even now planning to appear in Fudge's office and vanish him for trying to help the other side - whoever they were?

          And then - one Tuesday -

*An early draft of
Harry Potter and the
Philosopher's Stone*

J.K. ROWLING

Later that evening, when everyone else had gone home, Dursley sneaked pp to Fudge's office carrying a crib., which he laid on Fudge's desk.

The child was asleep. Fudge peered nervously into the crib. The boy had a cut on his forehead. It was a very strangely shaped cut. It looked like a bolt of lightening.

"Going to leave a scar, I expect," said Fudge.

"Never midd the ruddy scar, what are we going to do with him?" said Dursley.

"Do with him? Why, you 'll have to take him home, of course," said Fudge in surprise. "He's your nephew. His parents have banished. What else can we do? I thought you didn't want anyone to know you had relatives involved in all these odd doings?"

"Take him home!" said Dursley in horror. "My son Didsbury is just this age, I don't want him coming in contact with one of these."

"Very well, then, Dursley, we shall just have to try and fin someone who does want to take him. Of course, it will be difficult to keep the story out of the press. Noenne else has lived after one of these vanishments. There'll be a lot of interest -"

"Oh, very <u>well</u>," snapped Dursley. "I'll take him."

He picked up the crib and stumped angrily from the room.

Fudge closed his briefcase. It was time he was getting home too. He had just put his hand on the doorhandle when a low cough behind him made him clap his hand to his heart.

"Don't hurt me! I'm a Muggle! I'm a Muggle!"

"I know yeh are," said a low, growling voice.

It was the giant.

"You!" said Fudge. "What is it? Oh, Good Lord, don't tell me-" For the giant, he saw, was crying. Sniffing into a large spotted handkerchief.

"It's all over," said the giant.

"Over?" said Fudge faintly, "It didn't work? Has he killed Dunderbore? Are we all going to be turned into slaves?"

"No, no," sobbed the giant. "He's gone. Everyone's come back. Diggle, the Bones, the McKinnons... they're all back. Safe. Everyone 'e took is back on our side an' He's disappeared 'imself."

"Good Heavens! This is wonderful news! You mean Mr. Dunderbumble's plan worked?"

eyes. "Never 'ad a chance to try it," said the giant, mopping his

# HARRY ARRIVES AT PRIVET DRIVE

'While you can still call home the place where your mother's blood dwells, there you cannot be touched or harmed by Voldemort. He shed her blood, but it lives on in you and her sister. Her blood became your refuge. You need return there only once a year, but as long as you can still call it home, whilst you are there he cannot hurt you ...'

PROFESSOR DUMBLEDORE – HARRY POTTER AND THE ORDER OF THE PHOENIX

THIS ORIGINAL DRAWING by J.K. Rowling shows the scene when Harry Potter was delivered to the Dursleys. Hagrid, still wearing his motorcycle goggles, stoops down to show Dumbledore and Professor McGonagall the baby. Harry is the focus of this image, wrapped in a white blanket.

*Drawing of Harry Potter, Dumbledore, McGonagall and Hagrid by J.K. Rowling*

J.K. ROWLING

# THE MAGIC CIRCLE

Protective enchantments are used in the wizarding world to keep something safe. Hogwarts is protected by a Muggle-Repelling Charm. To Muggles the school simply looks like an old abandoned castle.

In this painting, John William Waterhouse (1849–1917) shows a woman drawing a protective circle around herself with a wand. Outside the magic circle, in a strange and empty landscape, are ravens, toads, and a skull half-buried in the ground. Within the protective circle we can see the glowing fire, flowers growing, and the woman in a beautifully vibrant dress.

 *John William Waterhouse, The Magic Circle (1886)*
TATE BRITAIN

*'If we're staying, we should put some protective enchantments around the place,' she replied, and raising her wand, she began to walk in a wide circle around Harry and Ron, murmuring incantations as she went. Harry saw little disturbances in the surrounding air: it was as if Hermione had cast a heat haze upon their clearing.*

HARRY POTTER AND THE DEATHLY HALLOWS

## ACTIVITY

### GHOST IN A BOTTLE

Fill a large, clear plastic bottle with cold water and add a few drops of orange food colouring. Ask an adult to help you cut across a thin, white plastic bag roughly 10 cm up from the bottom. This will make a 'mini bag'. Put a tablespoon of water in this and twist to make a water-filled 'head' (your ghost) and fasten with an elastic band. Draw a face on the head. Make sure the head will fit into the bottle! Cut the bottom of the ghost into shreds. Finally, put your ghost head-first into the bottle, replace the top and shake! Now watch your ghost fly...

# A Snake Charmer

Serpents feature prominently in the wizarding world of Harry Potter. Salazar Slytherin, the founder of Slytherin House at Hogwarts, Lord Voldemort and Harry Potter are all Parselmouths and can communicate with serpents; while Nagini, Lord Voldemort's snake and loyal servant, is a gigantic snake measuring at least twelve feet long.

---

*... he had shouted stupidly at the snake, 'Leave him!' And miraculously – inexplicably – the snake slumped to the floor, docile as a thick black garden hose, its eyes now on Harry.*

Harry Potter and the Chamber of Secrets

---

This image of a 'wizard' charming a serpent comes from a beautifully illustrated bestiary decorated with real gold. The text describes several mythological snakes, including the *cerastes* (a horned serpent). It also looks at the *emorroris*, a type of asp (a venomous snake). If bitten by the asp, the victim sweats out their own blood until they die.

However, the manuscript goes on to explain how the snake can be caught. To do this, a conjurer must sing to it, making it fall asleep. This allows the snake charmer (shown holding what might be a wand) to remove the precious stone that grows on the asp's forehead. The manuscript contains 80 other illustrations of real and mythical creatures, such as a phoenix, a unicorn and a centaur.

*Image of a snake charmer, in a bestiary (England, 13th century)*
BRITISH LIBRARY

## FACT

### WHAT IS A BESTIARY?

Bestiaries are beautifully illustrated books, which contain descriptions and stories about animals. The first ones were written in Ancient Greece, but they became popular in the Middle Ages. Bestiaries contained both real and mythical animals, so you might find information about dragons and unicorns as well as lions and bears!

# MAGICAL SERPENTS

Throughout history there have been people who believed that snakes were magical creatures. Because they can shed and regrow their skin, snakes are often associated with renewal, rebirth and healing. In many cultures they represent both good and evil.

*The snake suddenly opened its beady eyes. Slowly, very slowly, it raised its head until its eyes were on a level with Harry's. It winked.*

HARRY POTTER AND THE PHILOSOPHER'S STONE

This magic staff was carved from timber that had been buried for centuries in peat. Known as bog oak, the low oxygen levels, acidity and tannins of the peat preserved the wood, hardening and blackening it in the process. Carved by a man named Stephen Hobbs, and given to a Wiccan priest, Stewart Farrar (1916–2000), this staff was decorated with a serpent – it was believed it would enhance its power.

Below it is a wand that would have been used to channel magical forces. Its dark colour and snake-like shape might make us wonder whether it has been used for good or evil.

*A serpent staff*
THE MUSEUM OF WITCHCRAFT AND MAGIC

*A wand shaped like a snake*
THE MUSEUM OF WITCHCRAFT AND MAGIC

## DID YOU KNOW?

*It was believed that snakes could be used for both good and evil in magic. Powdered rattlesnake skin, or the rattle itself, was used in spells to bring good luck. Snakeskin was also meant to be able to reverse spells that cause madness. However, people believed that snake blood fed to an enemy would cause snakes to grow inside them. Spells like this have been used in North America and Latin America.*

## FACT

### WANDS AND MAGIC

Wands, staffs, rods and sceptres have long been associated with power. They were originally bundles of slim twigs used by priests to call spirits. In magic, wands are used to channel energy or spells. They can be made of different types of wood, which gives them different characteristics, and can have other plants, feathers, precious stones or metals bound to them to enhance their abilities.

# HARRY AND THE BASILISK

*Fawkes was soaring around its head, and the Basilisk was snapping furiously at him with fangs long and thin as sabres.*

HARRY POTTER AND THE CHAMBER OF SECRETS

IN THIS STRIKING IMAGE the giant Basilisk coils past Harry. The beast is so huge that it's hard to tell where its body begins and where it ends. The ruby-decorated sword of Godric Gryffindor is clutched in Harry's hands in mid-swing. The Basilisk's terrible yellow eyes are streaming with blood after Fawkes the phoenix has scratched them with his claws. The image appears in *Harry Potter and the Chamber of Secrets*.

*Harry Potter and the Basilisk*
*by Jim Kay*
BLOOMSBURY

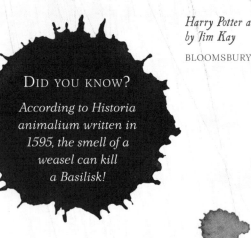

### DID YOU KNOW?

*According to Historia animalium written in 1595, the smell of a weasel can kill a Basilisk!*

# THE BASILISK

*The enormous serpent, bright, poisonous green, thick as an oak trunk, had raised itself high in the air and its great blunt head was weaving drunkenly between the pillars.*

HARRY POTTER AND THE CHAMBER OF SECRETS

A BRIEF DESCRIPTION *of the Nature of the Basilisk, or* Cockatrice *contains just three pages and was written by James Salgado. Around 1680 Salgado displayed a Basilisk (presumably in stuffed form) given to him by a Dutch doctor who had recently returned from Ethiopia.

He wrote this pamphlet to accompany the Basilisk, describing the beast as yellow, with a crown-like crest and a body like a cockerel's but with a serpent's tail. Salgado also wrote about the danger of the Basilisk's glare: 'In the time of Alexander the Great, there was one of them which, lying hid in a wall, killed a great troop of his soldiers by the poisonous glances of his eyes upon them.'

*A Brief Description of the Nature of the Basilisk, or Cockatrice (London, c. 1680)*
BRITISH LIBRARY

# ETHIOPIAN TALISMANS

*'... I remember something very similar happening in Ouagadougou,' said Lockhart, 'a series of attacks, the full story's in my autobiography. I was able to provide the townsfolk with various amulets which cleared the matter up at once ...'*

HARRY POTTER AND THE CHAMBER OF SECRETS

This magical recipe book (opposite) was made in Ethiopia in 1750. Written in a language called Ge'ez (also known as classic Ethiopic) it contains a huge collection of protective amulets, talismans and charms. This manuscript would have belonged to an exorcist (someone who gets rid of evil spirits) or a debtera.

Debteras are Ethiopian religious figures in some communities. They are trained to work as healers, fortune tellers and astrologers, and make amulets to protect people from evil spirits. They also put scarecrows in fields and treat people for headlice!

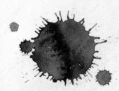

*An Ethiopian magical recipe book (1750)*
BRITISH LIBRARY

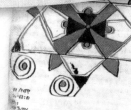

Debteras are known for producing amulet scrolls and practising traditional medicine. These pages contain illustrations of talismans and geometric images, which would have been used for making amulet scrolls, together with prayers for undoing spells and charms. Talismanic drawing focuses on the image of the eye, providing a defence against the dark arts.

# CARE OF MAGICAL CREATURES

> 'C'mon, now, get a move on!' he called, as the class approached. 'Got a real treat for yeh today! Great lesson comin' up!'

CARE OF MAGICAL CREATURES is an optional subject taught at Hogwarts, which Harry, Ron and Hermione first study in their third year. Students learn all about a wide range of magical creatures, from what they feed on and their breeding habits to what helps them thrive in the magical world. During each lesson a new and different species is studied, from Hippogriffs and Flobberworms to Blast-Ended Skrewts.

## FACT

### BELIEF IN MAGICAL CREATURES

Long ago, people really did believe in magical creatures. Earthquakes were believed to be caused by giants moving around underground and if children went missing near lakes, shape-shifting kelpies were blamed for stealing them.

Some creatures were probably just a misunderstanding of what people saw. For example mermaids could have been marine mammals called dugongs, which means 'lady of the sea'. These creatures hold their babies like humans and poke their heads out of the water. Draped in seaweed this might look like long hair from afar.

## RUBEUS HAGRID
## KEEPER OF KEYS AND GROUNDS

### PROFESSOR OF:
## CARE OF MAGICAL CREATURES

APPEARANCE: Half-giant with long tangles of bushy black hair and a beard that covers most of his face, Hagrid is huge. His hands are the size of dustbin lids and his feet are like baby dolphins!

DID YOU KNOW: Cats make Hagrid sneeze!

'Hagrid is a relief to draw because drawing children you can't put a line wrong, a misplaced scribble can age a child by ten years. There are no such problems with Hagrid: he's a mass of scribbles with eyes.'

JIM KAY, 2017

*A portrait of Hagrid by Jim Kay*

BLOOMSBURY

# A GIANT FROM UNDERGROUND

ATHANASIUS KIRCHER (1602–1680), author of *Mundus Subterraneus* ('The Underground World'), experienced an earthquake while travelling through Italy and became fascinated with what was beneath the ground. His interests even led him to climb inside the volcano Mount Vesuvius, which had last erupted only seven years earlier!

Kircher believed that beneath the Earth's surface the ground was full of empty spaces and hidden burrows and that these caverns contained many wonders, including dragons and even giants. Kircher claimed that an enormous skeleton of a giant had been discovered sitting in a Sicilian cave in the 14th century. This image shows the scale of that Sicilian giant in comparison with a normal human, the Biblical giant Goliath, a Swiss giant and a Mauritanian giant.

*A giant, in Athanasius Kircher, Mundus Subterraneus (Amsterdam, 1665)*

BRITISH LIBRARY

## FACT

### GIANTS

Almost every country has legends of giants. They were often believed to have built ancient monuments or natural features that no one could imagine humans having made, like Stonehenge (Wiltshire, England) or the Giant's Causeway (Northern Ireland).

# HAGRID AND HARRY AT GRINGOTTS

*They were going even deeper now and gathering speed. The air became colder and colder as they hurtled round tight corners.*

HARRY POTTER AND THE PHILOSOPHER'S STONE

In this original hand-drawn illustration by J.K. Rowling, Hagrid is taking Harry on his first trip to his vault at Gringotts, located in the highly protected caverns deep beneath the wizarding bank. The half-giant only just about fits inside the small cart and he covers his eyes with his hand as their cart zooms deep underneath the bank, while Harry, on the other hand, keeps his eyes wide open.

*Drawing of Harry and Hagrid at Gringotts by J.K. Rowling*

J.K. ROWLING

ton

epanum

cubitus

RIMA.

osæ magnitudinis

# TROLLS

THESE TYPED PAGES are from an unedited version of *Harry Potter and the Philosopher's Stone*. In this scene some passages were shortened during the editorial process.

This text contains a slightly different account of Ron and Harry coming face-to-face with a troll in the girls' bathroom than that which appears in the published version.

"Hello, hello," he said absently, "Just pondering a little problem, don't take any notice of me..."

"What's Peeves done this time?" asked Harry.

"No, no, it's not Peeves I'm worried about," said Nearly Headless Nick, looking thoughtfully at Harry. "Tell me, Mr. Potter, if you were

167

worried that someone was up to something they shouldn't be, would you tell someone else, who might be able to stop it, even if you didn't think much of the person who might be able to help?"

"Er - you mean - would I go to Snape about Malfoy, for instance?"

"Something like that, something like that...."

"I don't think Snape would help me, but it'd be worth a try, I suppose," said Harry curiously.

"Yes... yes... thank you, Mr. Potter..."

Nearly Headless Nick glided away. Harry and Ron watched him go, puzzled looks on their faces.

"I suppose you're bound not to make much sense if you've been beheaded," said Ron.

Quirrell was late for class. He rushed in looking pale and anxious and told them to turn to "p-page fifty four" at once, to look at "t-t-trolls."

"N-now, who c-c-can tell me the three types of t-troll? Yes, Miss G-

167

Granger?"

"Mountain-dwelling, river-dwelling and sea-dwelling," said Hermione promptly. "Mountain-dwelling trolls are the biggest, they're pale grey, bald, have skin tougher than a rhinoceros and are stronger than ten men. However, their brains are only the size of a pea, so they're easy to confuse -"

"Very g-good, thank you, Miss Gr -"

"River trolls are light green and have stringy hair -"

"Y-y-yes, thank you, that's excell -"

" - and sea trolls are purplish grey and -"

"Oh, someone shut her up," said Seamus loudly. A few people laughed.

There was a loud clatter as Hermione jumped to her feet, knocking her chair over, and ran out of the room with her face in her hands. A very awkward silence followed.

"Oh d-d-dear," said Professor Quirrell.

*

When Harry woke up next day, the first thing he noticed was a delicious smell in the air.

"It's pumpkin, of course!" said Ron, "Today's Hallowe'en!"

Harry soon realised that Hallowe'en at Hogwarts was a sort of mini-Christmas. When they got down to the Great Hall for breakfast, they found that it had been decorated with thousands of real bats, which were hanging off the ceiling and window-sills, fast asleep. Hagrid was putting hollow pumpkins on all the tables.

"Big feast tonight," he grinned at them, "See yeh there!"

There was a holiday feeling in the air because lessons would be finishing early. No-one was in much of a mood for work, which annoyed Professor McGonagall.

168

"Unless you settle down, you won't be going to the feast at all," she said, a few minutes into Transfiguration. She stared at them until they had all fallen silent. Then she raised her eyebrows.

"And where is Hermione Granger?"

They all looked at each other.

"Miss Patil, have you seen Miss Granger?"

Parvati shook her head.

cupboard doors, but not a hint of a troll did they find.

They'd just decided to try the dungeons when they heard footsteps.

"If it's Snape, he'll send us back - quick, behind here!"

They squeezed into an alcove behind a statue of Godfrey the Gormless.

Sure enough, a moment later they caught a glimpse of Snape's hook nose rushing past. Then they heard him whisper "Alohomora!" and a click.

"Where's he gone?" Ron whispered.

"No idea - quick, before he gets back -"

They dashed down the stairs, three at a time, and rushed headlong into the cold darkness of the dungeons. They passed the room where they usually had Potions and were soon walking through passages they'd never seen before. They slowed down, looking around. The walls were wet and slimey and the air was dank.

"I never realised they were so big," Harry whispered as they turned yet another corner and saw three more passageways to choose from. "It's like Gringotts down here..."

173

Ron sniffed the damp air.

"Can you smell something?"

Harry sniffed too. Ron was right. Above the generally musty smell of the dungeons was another smell, which was rapidly becoming a foul stench, a mixture of old socks and public toilets, the concrete kind that no-one seems to clean.

And then they heard it. A low grunting - heavy breathing - and the shuffling footfalls of gigantic feet.

They froze - they couldn't tell where the sound was coming from amid all the echoes -

Ron suddenly pointed; at the end of one of the passageways,

*A typed draft of Harry Potter and the Philosopher's Stone by J.K. Rowling*

J.K. ROWLING

something huge was moving. It hadn't seen them... it ambled out of sight...

"Merlin's beard," said Ron softly, "It's enormous..."

They looked at each other. Now that they had seen the troll, their ideas of fighting it seemed a bit - stupid. But neither of them wanted to be the one to say this. Harry tried to look brave and unconcerned.

"Did you see if it had a club?" Trolls, he knew, often carried clubs. Ron shook his head, also trying to look as though he wasn't bothered.

"You know what we should do?" said Harry, "Follow it. Try and lock it in one of the dungeons - trap it, you know..."

If Ron had been hoping Harry was going to say, "Let's go back to the feast", he didn't show it. Locking up the troll was better than trying to fight it.

"Good idea," he said.

They crept down the passageway. The stench grew stronger as they reached the end. Very slowly, they peered around the corner.

174

There it was. It was shuffling away from them. Even from the back, it was a horrible sight. Twelve feet tall, its skin was a dull, granite grey, its great lumpy body like a boulder with its small bald head perched on top like a coconut. It had short legs thick as tree trunks with flat, horny feet. The smell coming from it was incredible. It was holding a huge wooden club, which dragged along the floor because its arms were so long.

They pulled their heads back out of sight.

"Did you see the size of that club?" Ron whispered. Neither of them could have lifted it.

"We'll wait for it to go into one of the chambers and then barricade the door," said Harry. He looked back around the corner.

The troll had stopped next to a doorway and was peering inside. Harry could see its face now; it had tiny red eyes, a great squashed nose and a gaping mouth. It also had long, dangling ears which waggled as it shook its head, making up its tiny mind where to go next. Then it slouched slowly into the chamber.

Harry looked around, searching -

"There!" he whispered to Ron, "See? On the wall there!"

A long, rusty chain was suspended about half way down the passageway. Harry and Ron darted forward and pulled it off its nail. Trying to stop it clinking, they tiptoed towards the open door, praying the troll wasn't about to come out of it -

Harry seized the door handle and pulled it shut: with trembling hands, they looped the chain around the handle, hooked it onto a bolt sticking out of the wall and pulled it tight.

"It'll take it a while to get out of that," Harry panted, as they pulled the chain back across the door and tied it firmly to a torch bracket,

"Come

175

on, let's go and tell them we've caught it!"

Flushed with their victory they started to run back up the passage, but as they reached the corner they heard something that made their hearts stop - a high, petrified scream - and it was coming from the chamber they'd just chained up -

"Oh, no," said Ron, pale as the Bloody Baron.

"There's someone in there!" Harry gasped.

"*Hermione!*" they said together.

It was the last thing they wanted to do, but what choice did they have? Wheeling around they sprinted back to the door and ripped the chain off, fumbling in their panic - Harry pulled the door open - they ran inside.

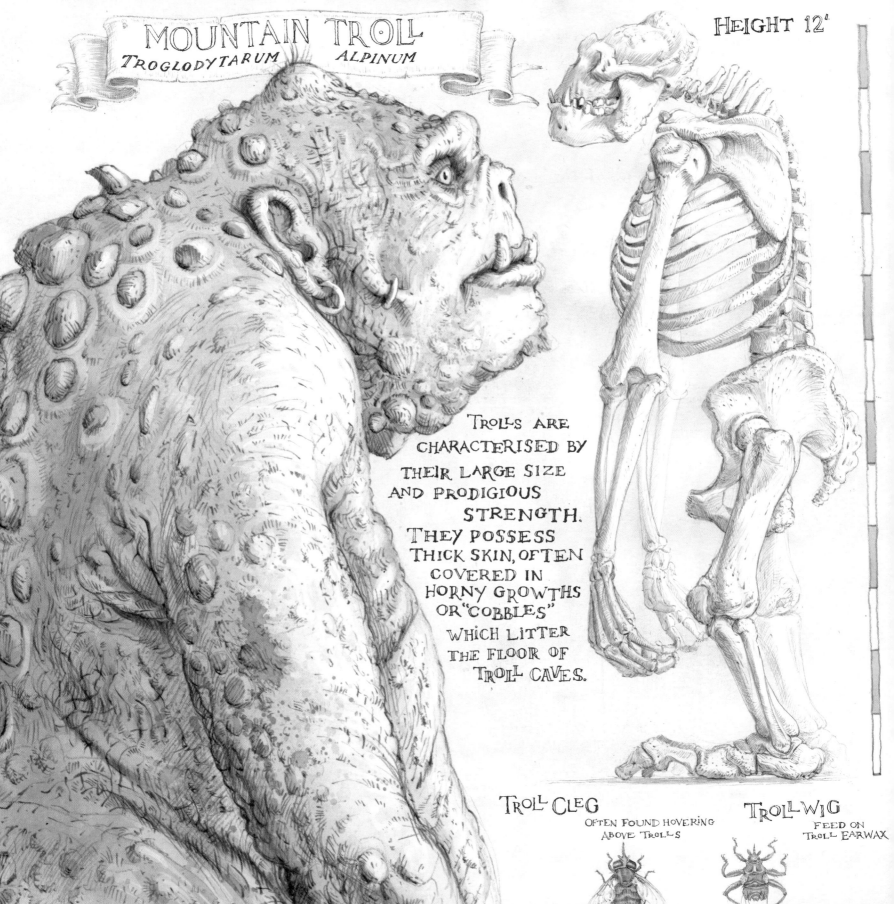

# MOUNTAIN TROLL
*TROGLODYTARUM ALPINUM*

HEIGHT 12'

TROLLS ARE CHARACTERISED BY THEIR LARGE SIZE AND PRODIGIOUS STRENGTH. THEY POSSESS THICK SKIN, OFTEN COVERED IN HORNY GROWTHS OR "COBBLES" WHICH LITTER THE FLOOR OF TROLL CAVES.

TROLL CLEG
OFTEN FOUND HOVERING ABOVE TROLLS

TROLLWIG
FEED ON TROLL EARWAX

# A Mountain Troll

*It was a horrible sight. Twelve feet tall, its skin was a dull, granite grey, its great lumpy body like a boulder with its small bald head perched on top like a coconut. It had short legs thick as tree trunks with flat, horny feet.*

HARRY POTTER AND THE PHILOSOPHER'S STONE

THIS IMAGE SHOWS a study of a mountain troll by Jim Kay. The artist has included a scientific name for the troll – *Troglodytarum Alpinum*. The creature is covered in growths and has a vacant look on its face.

### DID YOU KNOW?

*The term 'troll' originates from Old Norse, the creatures having first appeared in Scandinavian folklore. The word 'trow' also comes from 'troll', although it actually refers to very different beings: fairies or hidden people in the Shetlands.*

*Drawing of a mountain troll by Jim Kay*

BLOOMSBURY

# A Toxic Toad

From predicting the weather to bringing good luck and being used for cures, toads have appeared in magical folklore for hundreds of years. The cane toad, or giant marine toad, is the world's largest toad. It has unwebbed hands and feet, brown-coloured irises and its venom glands, which are dotted across the surface of its skin, produce a toxic milky substance. It is one of the many creatures described by famous German biologist, Johann Baptist von Spix (1781–1826).

*J. B. von Spix, Animalia nova, sive species novæ testitudinum et ranarum, quas in itinere per Brasiliam annis 1817–1820 ... collegit, et descripsit (Munich, 1824)*

BRITISH LIBRARY

BUFO Agua.
Le Crapaud Agua.
Tab: XV.

# ESCAPE FROM GRINGOTTS

THIS IS THE FIRST handwritten draft of the scene in *Harry Potter and the Deathly Hallows*, in which Harry, Ron and Hermione escape from Gringotts on the back of a dragon. The first page describes this dramatic escape, while the page on the right-hand side describes Harry destroying a cup (the Hufflepuff Horcrux) while they are still in the Lestranges' vault, an event that changed for the published book.

This handwritten draft shows how the scenes in the books were not necessarily written in order, and that some of them were later re-written. There are lots of crossings-out, arrows and little sentences in the margins and one of Harry's lines is represented by a cross on the second page, which we can assume meant that it would be filled in at a later stage.

*An early draft of Harry Potter and the Deathly Hallows by J.K. Rowling*

J.K. ROWLING

sword ~~and~~ seized Griphook's hand and
pulled. The blistered, howling Goblin
emerged by degrees.

'~~Hermione~~ ~~let me down!~~ ~~they yelled,~~

'X' yelled Harry and he landed on the
bumpy surface of the ~~the~~ smelling treasure
~~with~~ ~~the goblin~~ on his shoulder again,
now ~~a all crowd~~ ~~a hundred~~ ~~of himself again,~~ but
Gryffindor ~~multiplying~~ ~~there~~ swords of
~~multiplying~~ were multiplying all
around him.

'The real one —' he ~~roared~~: ~~to~~
~~they~~ had to destroy the Horcrux, ~~if~~ 'where—
it's got the cup on 'it —'

~~And then it was~~

The jewelled hilt was shoved into
his hand: Griphook had spotted and seized it. In one
fluid action, too ~~that~~ the air, hot
~~gets~~ screams, ~~and it~~ Harry swung
~~raised~~ the sword into the air ~~swung the he~~
up, turned over and fell, ~~Harry~~ the cup flew
into the air and he impaled it on the blade
~~descent, so that~~ the point of the sword
penetrating the bottom of the cup.

~~There was a~~

He heard no sound, but a bloodlike
liquid gushed from the punctured cup,
splashing over ~~all Hermione~~ who choked and gasped, and then
they were sliding uncontrollably out of
the vault on a great mass of gold and
silver: the waiting goblins had removed
the door ~~again~~.
~~The treasure~~
~~there was~~ only                     in Harry's head
Harry ~~as~~ had only one thought; goblins
did not carry wands.

# THE BOLOGNA DRAGON

On 13 May 1572, it was said that a 'monstrous dragon' was found in the countryside near Bologna, Italy. The discovery was seen as a bad omen, and so the dragon's body was given to the celebrated naturalist and collector Ulisse Aldrovandi (1522–1605), to examine. Aldrovandi's findings appear in *A History of Snakes and Dragons*, which provides detailed descriptions of snakes, dragons and other monsters, explaining their temperament and habitat.

*Ulisse Aldrovandi,*
*Serpentum et Draconum*
*Historiae (Bologna, 1640)*
BRITISH LIBRARY

### Did you know?

*The Bologna Dragon might sound like a hoax but Aldrovandi was a respected naturalist who made careful notes and drawings of a two-legged reptile. We can't know for sure what he actually saw but two-legged reptiles do exist and perhaps Aldrovandi's dragon was a related species but is now extinct ...*

# DRAGON EGGS

This image of dragon eggs by Jim Kay contains a wide variety of species. To create the image the artist drew and coloured the different shapes and base colours of the eggs. He added extra details and flecks of colours and included the writing digitally to create the final images. The scale to indicate the size of the eggs shows that the smallest egg was around six inches high (the same size as an ostrich egg) and the largest was up to 15 inches. Some of these eggs are deceptively ordinary, while others belong unmistakably to the magical world.

## ACTIVITY

### MAKE YOUR OWN DRAGON EGG

Ask an adult to help you hard boil an egg, then let it cool for ten minutes. Mix together a teaspoon of gel food colouring and two tablespoons of white wine vinegar in a small bowl. Put the warm egg into the mixture – it won't cover it, but don't worry. Leave for ten minutes, then turn the egg over, so another part gets dyed. Repeat once more, then add four tablespoons of hot water to the colouring. Let the egg sit in the diluted colouring for 30 minutes, turning once or twice, then let it dry on a kitchen towel. The end result will be an impressively splodgy dragon egg!

*Final image of dragon eggs by Jim Kay*
BLOOMSBURY

# DRAGON EGGS

FROM "DRAGON-BREEDING FOR PLEASURE AND PROFIT"

HUNGARIAN HORNTAIL

UKRANIAN IRONBELLY

ANTIPODEAN OPALEYE

INCHES

SWEDISH SHORT-SNOUT

PERUVIAN VIPERTOOTH

CHINESE FIREBALL

HEBRIDEAN BLACK

ROMANIAN LONGHORN

NORWEGIAN RIDGEBACK

COMMON WELSH GREEN

# Nearly Headless Nick

The Spirit Division is one of three parts of the Department for the Regulation and Control of Magical Creatures. The other two parts are the Beast Division and the Being Division; it also incorporates the Goblin Liaison Office and Pest Advisory Bureau.

This hand-drawn image of Nearly Headless Nick by J.K. Rowling shows the Gryffindor ghost demonstrating exactly how you can be nearly headless. This must be an early image of Nearly Headless Nick, or Sir Nicholas de Mimsy-Porpington to give him his proper name, as he is not wearing the ruff familiar to Gryffindor students.

*Drawing of Nearly Headless Nick by J.K. Rowling (1991)*

J.K. ROWLING

# Peeves the Poltergeist

This hand-drawn image by J.K. Rowling shows the Hogwarts poltergeist, Peeves, in his visible form; he is able to become invisible at will. A poltergeist (meaning 'noisy ghost' in German) is generally understood to be an evil spirit, which creates a physical disturbance.

*Drawing of Peeves by J.K. Rowling (1991)*

J.K. ROWLING

*Nearly Headless Nick by Jim Kay*

BLOOMSBURY

## FACT

### GHOSTS AND POLTERGEISTS

Poltergeists are supposed to move objects and make unexplained noises. Apparently, the Thornton Road poltergeist in Birmingham threw stones at windows when no one was nearby.
Ghosts are meant to be the spirit of a dead person (or animal), which haunt different places. In cold weather, people have claimed to see the ghost of a chicken wandering around Pond Square in London!

# BUCKBEAK THE HIPPOGRIFF

*The first thing they saw on entering Hagrid's cabin was Buckbeak, who was stretched out on top of Hagrid's patchwork quilt, his enormous wings folded tight to his body, enjoying a large plate of dead ferrets.*

HARRY POTTER AND THE PRISONER OF AZKABAN

IN THIS IMAGE BY JIM KAY, Buckbeak the Hippogriff has taken over his owner's bed, his snack of dead ferrets close by. The interior of Hagrid's cabin was based on the real-life gardener's hut at Calke Abbey in Derbyshire. The blue highlights in the image echo the famous bluebells that are found at the abbey.

*Buckbeak the Hippogriff by Jim Kay*
BLOOMSBURY

## FACT

The word 'Hippogriff' combines the Ancient Greek words for horse and griffin. The beast was first described by the Italian poet Ludovico Ariosto (1474–1533) in his poem *Orlando Furioso*. Legend has it that the griffin, with an eagle's head and a lion's hindquarters, is an ancestor of the hippogriff.

# AN OUTSTANDING OWL

Although owls in the wizarding world are not magical, they are favoured pets because they can be used as carrier birds. Snowy owls are native to the Arctic regions of North America and Eurasia (the combined landmass of Europe and Asia). This hand-coloured and life-sized illustration of a pair of snowy owls appears in the enormous *Birds of America*, the first book to illustrate every bird native to North America. The illustrator, John James Audubon (1785–1851), chose to depict all the birds at their actual size.

*The snowy owl, in John James Audubon,*
*The Birds of America (London, 1827–38)*
BRITISH LIBRARY

# 'Was That A Mermaid?'

In this deleted chapter from *Harry Potter and the Chamber of Secrets*, Harry and Ron crash their enchanted Ford Anglia into the lake at Hogwarts instead of the Whomping Willow. They are saved by the merpeople, who flip the car over and drag it to safety.

This early draft shows one of the mermaids speaking to Harry and Ron in English, above the surface of the water. In the published books the characteristics of the merpeople have developed, and they are only ever seen to speak Mermish.

*The deleted merpeople chapter by J.K. Rowling, from Harry Potter and the Chamber of Secrets*

BLOOMSBURY

## Merpeople

*In* Fantastic Beasts and Where to Find Them, *the wizarding world's famed Magizoologist Newt Scamander noted some interesting things about merpeople. Also known as sirens, selkies or merrows, merpeople remain hidden. Muggle-Repelling Charms prevent trespassers from discovering the lakes and rivers in which they dwell. Merpeople speak Mermish and, like centaurs, requested 'beast' rather than 'being' status.*

---

*I wondered whether the mer-people scene actually works? After all, we don't see them again... What if, as an alternative, the car suddenly develops underwater troubles or something — and suddenly shoots out of the water? Might help [...]* — too!

...**"Oh, well - a fish -"** said Harry, **"A fish isn't going to do anything to us... I thought** it might be the giant squid."

There was a pause in which Harry wished he hadn't thought about the giant squid.

"There's loads of them," said Ron, swivelling round and gazing out of the rear window.

Harry felt as though tiny spiders were crawling up his spine. Large dark shadows were circling the car.

"If it's just fish..." he repeated.

And then, into the light, swam something Harry had never expected to see as long as he lived.

It was a woman. A cloud of blackest hair, thick and tangled like seaweed, floated all around her. Her lower body was a great, scaly fishtail the colour of gun-metal; ropes of shells and pebbles hung about her neck; her skin was a pale, silvery grey and her eyes, flashing in the headlights, looked dark and threatening. She gave a powerful flick of her tail and sped into the darkness.

"Was that a *mermaid*?" said Harry.

"Well, it wasn't the giant squid," said Ron.

There was a crunching noise and the car suddenly shifted.

Harry scrambled about to press his face against the back window. About ten merpeople, bearded men as well as long haired women, were straining against the car, their tails swishing behind them.

"Where are they going to take us?" said Ron, pannicking.

The mermaid they had seen first rapped on the window next to Harry and made a circular motion with her silvery hand.

"I think they're going to flip us over," said Harry quickly, "Hold on -"

They grabbed the door hands and slowly, as the mer-people pushed and strained, the car turned right over onto its wheels, clouds of silt fogging the water. Hedwig was beating her wings furiously against the bars of her cage again.

The mer-people were now binding thick, slimy ropes of lakeweed around the car and tying the ends around their own waists. Then, with Harry and Ron sitting in the front seats hardly daring to breathe, they pulled... the car was lifted off the bottom and rose, towed by the mer-people, to the surface.

"Yes!" said Ron, as they saw the starry sky again through their drenched windows.

The mer-people in front looked like seals, their sleek heads just visible as they towed the car towards the bank. A few feet from the grassy bank, they felt the wheels touch the pebbly ground of the lake again. The mer-people sank out of sight. Then the first mermaid bobbed up at Harry's window and rapped on it. He unwound it quickly.

"We can take you no further," she said. She had a strange voice, it was both screechy and hoarse. "The rocks are sharp in the shallows, but legs are not so easily torn as fins..."

"No," said Harry, nervously, "Look, we can't thank you enough..."

The mermaid gave a little flick of her tail and was gone.

"Come on, I need food..." said Ron, who was shivering.

They opened the doors of the car with difficulty, picked up Hedwig and Scabbers, braced themselves and jumped down into the freezing water, which came up above Harry's thighs. They waded to the bank and climbed out.

"Not as pretty as they look in books, are they, mermaids?" said Ron, trying to wring out his jeans. "Of course, they were lake people... maybe in a warm sea..."

Harry didn't answer; he was having trouble with Hedwig, who had clearly had enough of wizard transport. He let her out of her cage and she soared off at once towards a high tower which housed all the school owls.

# Bird-Eating Spiders

Maria Sibylla Merian (1647–1717) was a naturalist and zoological illustrator, celebrated for her groundbreaking work on South American insects. Between 1699 and 1701, Merian worked in Suriname (on the north-east coast of South America), where she made the drawings for the book from which the image below is taken. Many of the insects Merian discovered on her expedition had never been seen before by Europeans. When she published this image of a giant, bird-eating spider, people thought she had made it up. It was not until 1863 that the existence of this spider was finally accepted.

*Maria Sibylla Merian, Metamorphosis Insectorum Surinamensium (Amsterdam, 1705)*
BRITISH LIBRARY

# Ron and Harry Meet Aragog

*And from the middle of the misty domed web, a spider the size of a small elephant emerged, very slowly. There was grey in the black of his body and legs, and each of the eyes on his ugly, pincered head was milky white. He was blind.*

HARRY POTTER AND THE CHAMBER OF SECRETS

Jim Kay's image of the gigantic Aragog captures every terrifying detail of the spider who Harry and Ron meet in the Forbidden Forest in *Harry Potter and the Chamber of Secrets*. In the background, hundreds of spiders' legs become indistinguishable from the spiky trees, and the strands of the spiders' webs gleam white in Harry's wandlight.

### Did you know?

*Maria was 52 when she set out for Suriname with her 21-year-old daughter Dorothea. For two women to do this in 1699 was extraordinary. At the time women were expected to stay at home and look after the family.*

*Aragog by Jim Kay*
BLOOMSBURY

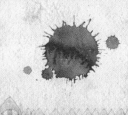

THE PHOENIX LIVES TO AN IMMENSE AGE AS
IT CAN REGENERATE, BURSTING INTO FLAMES
WHEN ITS BODY BEGINS TO FAIL AND RISING
AGAIN FROM THE ASHES AS A CHICK.

*The phoenix by Jim Kay*

BLOOMSBURY

# Fawkes the Phoenix

*A crimson bird the size of a swan had appeared, piping its weird music to the vaulted ceiling. It had a glittering golden tail as long as a peacock's and gleaming golden talons, which were gripping a ragged bundle.*

Harry Potter and the Chamber of Secrets

Jim Kay's glorious painting of a phoenix captures the brilliant colours of the bird's feathers. The phoenix has a piercing brown eye, bright blue claws and orange-red feathers, with an impressively long tail, much like a bird-of-paradise.

# Rising from The Flames

This 13th-century bestiary describes and illustrates the 'Fenix'. According to the text, the phoenix is so-called either because its colour is 'Phoenician purple' or because it is unique. It lives in Arabia and can live for 500 years. The phoenix's most remarkable feature is its ability to resurrect itself in old age. It creates a fire using a mound of branches and plants, and fans the flames with its own wings. The fire then consumes the bird. After nine days, it rises from the ashes.

*The phoenix in a medieval bestiary (England, 13th century)*
BRITISH LIBRARY

# THE PHOENIX

# PAST, PRESENT, FUTURE

> *The last trace of steam evaporated in the autumn air. The train rounded a corner. Harry's hand was still raised in farewell.*

HARRY POTTER AND THE DEATHLY HALLOWS

SINCE THE PUBLICATION of *Harry Potter and the Philosopher's Stone* in 1997, Harry Potter has delighted fans the world over. Following that time, J.K. Rowling has written three companion volumes in aid of charity – *Quidditch Through the Ages, Fantastic Beasts and Where to Find Them* and *The Tales of Beedle the Bard* – and has also collaborated on the play *Harry Potter and the Cursed Child Parts One and Two*, as well as writing the screenplay for *Fantastic Beasts and Where to Find Them*. Here we take a look at the now famous journey of the boy wizard and what the future holds …

## ILLUSTRATED PHILOSOPHER'S STONE

This unique first edition of *Harry Potter and the Philosopher's Stone* (opposite) contains drawings and annotations by J.K. Rowling. It was sold at a charity auction in 2013 in aid of English PEN and Lumos. There are 20 original illustrations by the author in the book, including a swaddled Harry Potter on the Dursleys' doorstep, a menacing Professor Snape, and an annotated sketch of the Hogwarts coat of arms. Forty-three pages in total contain notes or illustrations – in the annotations, J.K. Rowling reflects on and references the Harry Potter series and films. On the title page, she has written the simple words, *'changed my life forever'.*

### Harry Potter and the Philosopher's Stone

J. K. Rowling

*I remember practising my new signature, having added a 'K' at my publisher's request. It's here for my late and truly lamented paternal grandmother Kathleen, who listened to me making up stories with every appearance of delight + interest. God bless her.*

BLOOMSBURY

# Harry Potter and the Philosopher's Stone

*changed my life forever.*

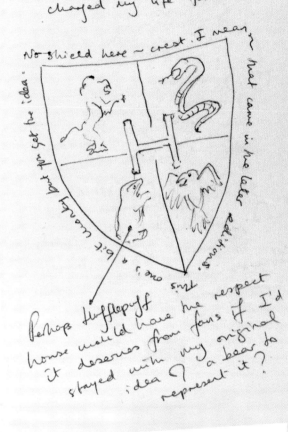

No shield here ~ crest. I mean... that came in the later editions but for get the idea.

Perhaps Huffleypuff house would have the respect it deserves from fans if I'd stayed with my original idea? a bear to represent it?

18     HARRY POTTER

corner he stopped and took out the silver Put-Outer. He clicked it once and twelve balls of light sped back to their street lamps so that Privet Drive glowed suddenly orange and he could make out a tabby cat slinking around the corner at the other end of the street. He could just see the bundle of blankets on the step of number four.

'Good luck, Harry,' he murmured. He turned on his heel and with a swish of his cloak he was gone.

A breeze ruffled the neat hedges of Privet Drive, which lay silent and tidy under the inky sky, the very last place you would expect astonishing things to happen. Harry Potter rolled over inside his blankets without waking up. One small hand closed on the letter beside him and he slept on, not knowing he was special, not knowing he was famous, not knowing he would be woken in a few hours' time by Mrs Dursley's scream as she opened the front door to put out the milk bottles, nor that he would spend the next few weeks being prodded and pinched by his cousin Dudley ... he couldn't know that at this very moment, people meeting in secret all over the country were holding up their glasses and saying in hushed voices: 'To Harry Potter – the boy who lived!'

Harry Potter rolled over inside his blankets without waking

106     HARRY POTTER

out that grubby little package. Had that been what the thieves were looking for?

As Harry and Ron walked back to the castle for dinner, their pockets weighed down with rock cakes they'd been too polite to refuse, Harry thought that none of the lessons he'd had so far had given him as much to think about as tea with Hagrid. Had Hagrid collected that package just in time? Where was it now? And did Hagrid know something about Snape that he didn't want to tell Harry?

Snape, brooding on the unfairness of life

*Harry Potter and the Philosopher's Stone, illustrated and annotated by J.K. Rowling (c. 2013)*

PRIVATE OWNER

# PLANNING THE ORDER OF THE PHOENIX

THESE PLANS FOR the Order of the Phoenix show the complexity of the storylines, and how they were carefully intertwined. The charts acted as an early planning device for J.K. Rowling, with the titles and order of the chapters sometimes changing in the published versions.

*Plans for Harry Potter and the*
*Order of the Phoenix by J.K. Rowling*

J.K. ROWLING

'These plans date from around 2001/2. I had plotted the remainder of the series in a broad sense by the time I finished Philosopher's Stone. I knew roughly who was going to die and where, and that the story would culminate in the Battle for Hogwarts.'

J.K. ROWLING, 2017

*Plans for Harry Potter and the Order of the Phoenix — a handwritten planning chart with columns: NO, TIME, TITLE, PLOT, PROPHECY / Hall of Prophecy, Cho/Ginny, D.A., O.O.P, Snape / Harry + father, Hagrid + Grawp.*

| NO. | TIME | TITLE | PLOT | PROPHECY | CHO/GINNY | D.A. | O.P. | Harry/Dad/Snape | Hagrid & Grawp |
|---|---|---|---|---|---|---|---|---|---|
| 1 | Aug | Dudley Demented | Harry desperate for information - Contact - letters circumspect - desperate to rejoin Weasleys - Listening to news - Dudley showdown - meets Dementor - Mrs. Figg | I but badly informed - divide anyone can take - L.M. + Nac. casing joint. Vol plotting Bode tries Malfoy to put B. under Imperius | | | | | Still with giants |
| 2 | Aug | A Peck of Owls | Confused letters from Ministry - Harry to bed very worried - newspapers (D.P.'s) 'Missy' Slipkiss | " | | | | Mention of Snape obliquely by Aunt P. | Still with giants |
| 3 | Aug | The Auror's Guard | Moody, Tonks and Lupin turn up to take Harry to Grimmauld. Finish on entry to kitchen | " | | | | | Still with giants |
| 4 | Aug | 12, Grimmauld Place | (Percy) F+G planning Dinner + masses of information 'Missy Slipkiss' → Sirius explains Fudge's standpoint. Ginny cheeky + funny Mrs. W. worried George + V. House-elf + Hermione? | LM do put Bode/anyone from Dept Myst under Imperius if get chance | See plot | Meet for 1st time - explicit aims | | Snape not present - hint why | Still with giants |
| 5 | Aug | The Ministry of Magic | Interrogation - Mrs. Figg witness - Dumbledore too See entrance (Percy) Dept. of Mysteries | LM hanging around Min. on excellent terms with Fudge (puts Bode under) | | Still around | | | Still w. giants |
| 6 | Aug | Mrs. Weasley's Worst Fears | The clock - Mrs. W's premonitions of doom - Percy etc - 'Missy' S? ----- more info + discussion Hermione Ron + Hermione prefects House-elf + Hermione? | Bode is under/and under orders to proceed v. cautiously | Ginny here Ginny/Hermione/Tonks | around Sirius farewell until Xmas | | | Still with giants |

The plans also note where individual characters are at different stages in the book. For example, Hagrid is still with the giants for the first nine chapters and Harry is at the Department of Mysteries when he realises that prophecies are held there. In these plans, the secret student body that came together to practise Defence Against the Dark Arts is called the Order of the Phoenix (abbreviated to 'OofP'), while the official resistance, formed of a group of anti-Dark Arts wizards and witches, is called Dumbledore's Army (abbreviated to 'D.A.').

# THE TALES OF BEEDLE THE BARD

*To Miss Hermione Jean Granger, I leave my copy of* The Tales of Beedle the Bard, *in the hope that she will find it entertaining and instructive.*

HARRY POTTER AND THE DEATHLY HALLOWS

In 2008, AFTER THE FINAL HARRY POTTER title had been released, *The Tales of Beedle the Bard* was published in aid of the charity Lumos. In *The Deathly Hallows*, Dumbledore leaves his own copy of *The Tales of Beedle the Bard*, written in runes, to Hermione. It contains several bedtime fairy stories told widely in the magical world.

This copy of *The Tales of Beedle the Bard* was handwritten by J.K. Rowling, bound in leather and embellished with gemstones with special meaning. It also features small illustrations by J.K. Rowling, such as the tree stump featured in *Babbitty Rabbitty and her Cackling Stump*.

*The Tales of Beedle the Bard by J.K. Rowling*
PRIVATE OWNER

Babbitty Rabbitty
and her Cackling Stump

A long time ago, in a far
off land, there lived a foolish
King, who decided that he
alone should have the
power of magic.

The Tales of
Beedle the Bard
translated from the
original runes
by
JKRowling

# THE WARLOCK'S HAIRY HEART

THIS IS AN ORIGINAL HANDWRITTEN draft of one of the stories in *The Tales of Beedle the Bard*. It is one of four wizarding fairy stories written by J.K. Rowling to accompany *The Tale of the Three Brothers*.

This draft outlines the plot and captures the essence of the story, but it was extended for the published version. It shows an example of a wizard attempting to use Dark Magic to protect himself from human vulnerability. By rejecting his heart and starving it of love, the warlock's heart becomes 'savage' and leads him to tragedy.

## DID YOU KNOW?

*The Tale of the Three Brothers* is *another story that featured in* The Tales of Beedle the Bard. *It tells the story of three men who tried to outwit Death through the use of magical objects called the Deathly Hallows. Long a subject of debate, Harry and his friends discover that these objects really do exist.*

*But the hairy heart was stronger than he was, and refused to relinquish its hold upon his senses or to return to the coffin in which it had been locked for so long.*

THE TALES OF BEEDLE THE BARD

maiden ~~she~~ came to condole with the warlock's
mother ~~She was a most gifted this~~ ~~worked~~
~~upon his father's death.~~ The young witch was beautiful, and gifted, ~~and~~ and her
family had much gold. The warlock had no heart to
feel, yet he ~~imagined~~ could understand the man
who married such a maid, ~~for~~ whose beauty would
excite envy in other men, whose magic ~~could~~
~~assist~~ ~~enable~~ ~~ensure a comfortable life for~~
~~secure~~ the comfort of her husband, and whose gold
~~the~~ assist her husband's ambitions and whose gold
would ensure his comfort. /Coldly and deliberately,
he began to pay court to ~~her~~ the maid. She was both
fascinated and frightened.
    'You seem not to feel,' she said wonderingly.
~~Have you a heart?~~ 'If I thought you truly had
                                       a heart...'
    The warlock understood that a show of feeling
was necessary to secure her hand, so he returned,
for the first time in ~~so~~ many years, to the place
where he had locked up his heart.
    ~~He had forgotten~~
    The heart was smaller by far than he
remembered, and much hairier. Nevertheless he
removed it from its enchanted box and
replaced it within his own breast.
    But the heart had grown savage during their
long estrangement. ~~It had been desire without feeling~~
~~to ~~ ~~Angrily~~ It beat fast within him,
~~and through his veins~~ ~~flowed lust within~~
~~like poisoned wine~~ spreading and what it spread
he returned to the maid

*Draft of The Warlock's Hairy
Heart by J.K. Rowling*

J.K. ROWLING

PAST, PRESENT, FUTURE / 133

# HARRY POTTER AND THE CURSED CHILD SET MODEL

BASED ON AN original new story by J.K. Rowling, Jack Thorne and John Tiffany, *Harry Potter and the Cursed Child* is a play by Jack Thorne. It had its official premiere at the Palace Theatre, London, on 30 July 2016 and among the many awards it has received since then is the Olivier for Best Set Design. This model box shows an evocative and flexible set design, which is integral to the theatrical magic that takes place on stage. Model boxes such as this one, designed by Christine Jones, help the creative team to work out the crucial detail of staging a play – ultimately making Harry Potter's world come alive before the audience's eyes.

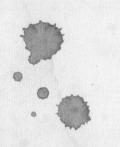

*Model box designed by Christine Jones with Brett J. Banakis, and built by Mary Hamrick, Amelia Cook, A Ram Kim, Amy Rubin and Kyle Hill*

*Original West End Company of Harry Potter and the Cursed Child at the Palace Theatre, London*

HARRY POTTER AND THE CURSED CHILD IS PRODUCED BY SONIA FRIEDMAN PRODUCTIONS, COLIN CALLENDER AND HARRY POTTER THEATRICAL PRODUCTIONS

# FANTASTIC BEASTS

*FANTASTIC BEASTS AND WHERE TO FIND THEM* was first published in 2001 under the name of Newt Scamander in aid of the charity Comic Relief. The following four images appear in the 2017 illustrated edition of the title. Illustrated by Olivia Lomenech Gill, each image portrays one of the wonderful creatures that Newt Scamander describes in his book. The Snallygaster is a half-bird, half-serpent creature with enormous wings, a long sharp beak and fierce claws. The Graphorn is an aggressive creature with a large humped back, two horns and four-thumbed feet. The Hodag is described as being the size of a large dog, having horns, red, glowing eyes and long fangs. The Hippogriff has the head of a giant eagle and the body of a horse and can be tamed, although this should only be attempted by experts.

*The Snallygaster*
*by Olivia Lomenech Gill*
BLOOMSBURY

*The Graphorn by Olivia Lomenech Gill*
BLOOMSBURY

*The Hodag*
*by Olivia Lomenech Gill*
BLOOMSBURY